Running Hot

Paul Youdelis

Published by Paul Youdelis, 2012.

RUNNING HOT

First edition. October 19, 2012.

Copyright © 2012 Paul Youdelis.

ISBN: 979-8224520657

Written by Paul Youdelis.

RUNNING HOT

Paul Youdelis

Published by Fat Guy Productions at Smashwords

Copyright 2012 Paul Youdelis

submitters will be able to review final text and assist in changes for accuracy. I want to take the opportunity to thank you all in advance for your help with this project. Be safe out there.

Captain Paul Youdelis

Clark County Fire Department, Station 12-C

p.s. Please forgive me if you happen to receive this message more than once. I am trying to contact as many fire fighters as possible. Gets kinda tough to keep track.

Chapter 1

"The young man had only the remaining shreds of a belt around his waist and as I looked to his feet....even his shoes were burned away."

SPRING HAS SPRUNG

Captain Bryan Perry - Station 11, A
City of Bakersfield, California

An eager, but elderly male picked up an attractive, young hooker and took her to the nearest and cheapest hotel. The old John was laying on his back receiving goods and services, with the energetic hooker straddling him. Unfortunately for the John, a bed spring in the mattress gave way, popping through the batting. The worn spring impaled, and screwd itself into the old guys butt cheek.

We were dispatched to the scene. On our arrival, we were met by several Bakersfield Police Department Officers who were having obvious difficulty controlling their laughter. We found the gentleman, stuck to the bed by his ass, in pain and obviously embarrassed. Our large bolt cutters were required to extricate him from the bed. The Gentleman was transported to the hospital on his stomach with a portion of the bed spring screwed, taped, and bandaged to his backside.

The disinterested hooker remained sitting in the corner of the room throughout the event. As we prepared to leave, the young woman added salt to the Johns wound, simply asking if she could "Use the room for the remainder of the evening".

THE WRONG PLACE
Captain Bryan Perry - Station 11, A
City of Bakersfield, California

While traveling down a dark, rural road in Bakersfield late one evening, I was startled by a large distant flash of light coming from the direction of the industrial area. My curiosity peeked, I decided to travel over and have a look. At the very least this could turn out to be a really cool fire to watch.

As I approached the area, I could see flames coming from the oil refinery, but what really caught my attention, in the middle of the road, walking, stumbling forward toward my truck, was the figure of a young man of about 25 years. His entire body was burned and smoking, his cloths burned away. The young man had only the remaining shreds of a leather belt around his waist and as I looked to his feet, I was horrified to note, that even his shoes were burned away.

A look of shock and dismay was on the young mans face. I parked and rushed over to him; He spoke first. "What happened?" He asked me. His face was burned so badly, that it looked almost translucent. His arms were burned in places to the bone and the seared flesh hung from his fingers. The dazed young man reached up with his disfigured hand and touched where his lips once were. There were second and third degree burns over his entire body. It was a miracle that this poor guy was alive, let alone able to talk.

Directly to the South, next to the rail road crossing guards, lay the smoking remains of what appeared to be a Camaro he had been driving. To the East, fire had engulfed the outbuildings of the refinery and to the West several oil tanks were split and spewing fire. The scene made little sense to me. All I could assume was that the young man had been caught in an explosion. The young man wondered aloud if he had been struck by a train as he slowed to a halt at the crossing.

Another passerby soon arrived and had a cell phone. I called our Emergency Communications Center and requested Emergency Medical Services (EMS), the Bakersfield Fire Departments Burn Team, and a 2 alarm response for the raging fire at the refinery. For the next 20 minutes, while waiting for EMS to arrive, I tried to talk to my patient. I was forced to keep him on his feet, as there was no place to lay him down except in dirt or cold, hard asphalt. I let him suck ice from the soda I had been carrying in my car. We talked about his family, his girlfriend and his young child.

It is odd to recall, that he was assuring me that he felt little pain, even though by now his feet were bleeding profusely. He asked me "Do I look pretty bad?" I didn't have the heart, and couldn't answer him..... He understood.

When the ambulance arrived, I helped the crew and we laid him into the burn sheets that the medics had placed over the gurney, as gently as we could. His head floated into the pillows closing his eyes for the last time. He asked me to call his girlfriend because she was expecting him and would be worried... he thanked me.

The State Fire Marshals Office determined the blast occurred when the young mans vehicle drove into an escaping vapor cloud, originating from one of the fuel oil storage tanks inside the refinery. An ignition source on the car ignited the fuel and a large fire ball engulfed the car - and the driver.

The refinery is gone now. Closed... then demolished. An overpass has been constructed to by-pass the rail lines that once stopped all traffic as they passed the gates to the refinery. All that remains of the event, along the side of the road is a square burned into the asphalt... about the size of a Camaro.

The memory of this young man will remain with me forever.

NOT QUITE DEAD YET

Communications Chief Charles Carter

Bossier City Fire Department, Bossier, Louisiana

Paul,

It is great to see that someone will write a book about fire fighters. We have always said we need to write a book about some of our experiences, but no one would ever believe us. Either it wouldn't be funny to them or they would think we were exaggerating. Here is one that just recently happened. I have some more firehouse stories that I will send you later if you want.

A 911 call came in for a medical problem over at the Bossier Parish Coroners Office. Needless to say, this was already an unusual call. The Coroners Office is pretty much at the end of the EMS chain. Anyhow, on arrival the crew found an 81 year old women, who was cold to the touch, but had a pulse, good blood pressure, and slow respirations.

The fire fighters loaded the elderly woman into the ambulance and she was transported across the street to the Christus Schumpert Bossier Hospital were she was said to be awake and talking.

It seems that the woman's home health nurse came to her house and found her, apparently dead. The nurse called her name, shook her, and even turned her over with no response. The nurse bypassed EMS, and instead called directly for the coroners office to respond. When the Coroner arrived, the woman was cold and pale, and he could detect no pulse.

The old gal was scooped up and transported to the Coroners office in a body bag. As preparations were being made to conduct an autopsy, it was discovered that the deceased in fact, wasn't! Four whole days, after being pronounced dead by the coroner, the dead is still alive and doing well.

GOOD INTENTIONS
Battalion Chief Gary McQueen - B Shift
Lake Oswego Fire & Rescue, Oregon
(A funny one. For reasons you will see, I won't mention the name of this Fire Department. I was not at this fire, but I heard about it directly from the person involved.)

A family had lost their house to a devastating fire. The fire fighters were in the overhaul stage when an Engineer heard a cat wailing. He searched through the brush and found this poor, badly burned cat. The animal was so seriously injured that the Engineer thought that the best thing to do was to put it out of its misery.

The Engineer looked around. After making sure nobody was watching, he picked up the cat and whacked its head on the front bumper of the engine. It didn't take a great blow, and the burnt cat went lifeless. The engineer laid the remains of the cat next to the bush where he found it and went back about his business.

A couple of months later, the grateful family came to visit the firefighters who had battled the blaze. They wanted to thank them for salvaging the things that they could, and to tell them how grateful they were to have such a caring organization of dedicated fire fighters. The conversation went on for a short while, then came the startling words... "And, by the way, The poor cat was so badly burned we didn't think he'd live, but we took him to the vet anyway and he's going to be just fine!"

(True story, Paul, I swear!)

Remember, fire fighters are just humans. While there actions might be well intended, there is no guaranteeing their methods.

THE JUMPER
Captain Lonnie Walch - Station 21, C Platoon
Clark County Fire Department, Las Vegas, Nevada

Our paramedic engine company was responding on a Code 1 (low priority) medical response when the dispatcher switched us to a different call, a report of a jumper at the Luxor Hotel and Casino. The odd part was that this jumper didn't leap off of the roof of a tall building, plunging to a grizzly death in the street below.

The Luxor is pyramid shaped and the rooms are on the outer part of the building with an open middle. This opening goes from the top of the building to the bottom where the casino, restaurants, and shops are located. This woman jumped to her death on the INSIDE of the building!

When we arrived we found the woman had jumped from the 25th floor. She landed near the buffet line, shooting skull pieces, brain fragments and other assorted chunks for some distance. The Hotel did a great job of immediately setting up counseling and debriefing for whoever needed it and eradicating the grisly scene.

A couple of days later we were running a medical call to the Luxor on the twenty-something floor. We looked down over the railing to see where the jumper had landed. It was easy to spot by the large patch of bright new carpet in the middle of the older, more faded carpet around it.

FRIENDS

Fire Fighter Richard Stone
James City County Fire Department, Williamsburg, Virginia

The call was for an amputated thumb. In the scope of things, this call sounded fairly routine. I was only an Explorer with the Department at the time and had just finished my EMT Class. My final exam was in two days, so riding the ambulance now was giving me good, needed experience.

As we went enroute, the dispatcher upgraded the call because the victim had lost consciousness. This upgrade added an engine company to the call as well. The call continued to spiral downward, going from routine to super stressful in the time it took the dispatchers to give us the next update. The dispatchers were now telling us that this was a 13 year old boy, and CPR was in progress. His heart had stopped beating.

We arrived to find the young boy at the top of the stairs. He was a bloody mess and was in full cardiac arrest. The boy had found directions to make a bomb on the internet using a small metal CO2 cartridge. He was in his room filling the cylinder with gun powder when the device blew up in his hand, indeed taking the boys thumb off. The explosion peppered the boy with shrapnel like shards from the CO2 cartridge. One piece of the sharp metal sliced into his chest - cutting his aorta.

There was no way for us in the field to know the true extent of the young mans injury. We started CPR at the top of the stairs in a small 4 foot square area. I was doing the chest compressions while the Paramedic started an IV, intubated the boy, and went through all the ALS protocols for a trauma code.

We put everything we had into this call and worked the boy for almost an hour. He was transported to the hospital and rushed into the Emergency Room. The E.R. Doctor called it when he saw the boys chest films and the damage to his aorta. There was nothing left to be done.

I remember the Paramedic filling out his report, asking if anyone got the boys name. I rattled off his full name as if it were my own. The Paramedic looked at me quizzically, wondering how I knew his name and said "Did you know him?" I did in fact know him. We had gone through Boy Scouts together and were close friends. The crew that was with me that day couldn't believe that I had been able to just get busy like that on a close friend, but what else could I do.

TROJAN
Battalion Chief Gary McQueen - B Shift
Lake Oswego Fire & Rescue, Oregon

OK, it has to happen every once in a while. The weird sex call. We got tapped out at about 0600 hours on a medical call. When we got on the air, the dispatcher gave us this information... "You are responding on a 32 year old female who has inhaled a prophylactic device." We couldn't believe what we had just heard, so in amazement, I asked her to repeat it, which she did. Nothing changed. "Holy shit!"

When we arrived, we were let in the house by a dressed man. He stated that his roommate had been "partying" with a young woman. The room showed signs of some serious activity. As he was walking us into the room, the involved male bailed out the front door, (some guy huh?) leaving this poor naked girl, that he picked up the night before, in his house full of Fire and Ambulance people!

Of course, she looked like a person who engages in this activity often, maybe even for a living.

She was sitting upright in the tripod position, crying and very frightened. She was afraid to swallow for fear of the condom blocking her airway, so drool was pouring from her mouth. We wrapped her up in a blanket and helped her to the gurney. She was transported to the hospital where, to make things worse, The Emergency Room Doctor couldn't find the rubber! In the end, she probably swallowed it and would pass it later.

SLEEPER SOFA

Captain Paul Youdelis - Station 12, C Platoon
Clark County Fire Department, Las Vegas, Nevada

I was just a rookie. I had only been on the job for a few months, and while I new I would see a lot on the job over the coming years, I didn't realize just how much I would see or how soon.

I was assigned to ride Rescue 14 for the Clark County Fire Department in Las Vegas, Nevada. Rescue 14 was one of the busier rescues in the County and still is to this day. Much of the area covered by 14 is low rent. My partner at the time was Paramedic Sean McManus. Sean had been on for a very long time, and had seen a lot, so I considered myself to be in pretty good hands.

We were dispatched around 13:00 hours for an unknown problem in one of our local mobile home parks. We flipped on our lights and sirens and headed over. On our arrival, we were met at the address by a neighbor. She told us that she didn't know what the problem was, but she could here someone in the home hoarsely and quietly calling out for help. She said that she had tried the door but found it locked.

Sean and I grabbed our med bags and walked up to the front door of the mobile home. Sure enough the door was locked. Inside, we could hear the raspy voice calling out for help. Sean told me to go around to the rear of the mobile home to try to find a way in, he would look for a way in from the front. I found no way in at the back, so I went around to the front and found that Sean had just finished jimmying the door with his Buck Knife.

I grabbed our gear and proceeded to follow Sean into the home. Sean stopped so suddenly, that I walked right into the back of him. I could not believe that we were looking at a naked man, trapped inside of a sleeper sofa.

To try to help you see what we saw, picture this in your mind...

Pull a folding bed out of a sofa. After you pull out the first level, you then take and unfold a foot section. If you take this open bed and remove the mattress, you find a springy chain link fence type device surrounded by a folding steel frame that the mattress rests on. This naked gentleman was laying on this sideways with no mattress and his head hanging over the side rail. The foot section was folded over the top of him, trapping him in between with his head hanging out of the side. Then take the whole works and shove it back into the sofa, with the arms of the sofa shoving his head up unmercifully.

The sofa was choking him and his voice was hoarse from calling out. We asked him how the hell this happened as we started to get him out. All he would say was he would tell us after we freed him. It took a few minutes and a bit of effort to get him out. His weight inside the sofa made it almost impossible to pull it out. The Ambulance had arrived and with their help we were able to free him from the clutches of the sofa.

After releasing him, while treating some minor injuries, he told us that he had been in there since 07:00 that morning. Over Six hours! He further told us that he and his girlfriend were into some kinky things. We replied "Your girlfriend left you folded in a sofa for over six hours?" He told us no, he was also into "Self abuse". It seems that he had folded himself into the foot part of the sofa for a rousing session of kinky masturbation, and in the throes of self passion the rest of the sofa folded in by itself, swallowing him up in the process.

WHEN YOU GOTTA GO
Anonymous

Early one morning a small town volunteer department was dispatched to a report of smoke coming from a building. Upon arrival, they found a commercial store front with apartments above and light to moderate smoke conditions inside. This was about 5:00 A.M.

While lines were being stretched, other fire fighters in full turnouts and SCBA entered the stairwell leading to the second floor apartments to start search and rescue. Meanwhile, other crews were sent to the roof with power saws to ventilate.

The interior search team came to the first apartment door and finding it locked, used brute force to open the door and start an interior search of the apartment. After a thorough search of the first apartment, and with smoke conditions becoming worse, they made their way down the increasingly smoke filled hallway to the second apartment door. They slammed their way through the doorway, only to find a very startled man and his wife sitting at the table eating breakfast.

When the couple asked why these fully clothed fire fighters had felt the need to break down their door, the residents were told the building was on fire, and they needed to evacuate immediately. To that, the woman replied, "I thought I saw smoke when I opened the cabinet to get the corn flakes". Her husband also remarked that he "wondered who the SOB was that was running his lawn mower at 5:00 in the morning". (the noise he was hearing was the crew on the roof cutting a ventilation hole with the power saws).

During this incident, the interior team had just finished clearing the attic, and noticed that one of their members was MIA (Missing in Action). There wasn't a lot of concern as the fire at this point had been knocked down, and crews were conducting overhaul. Light to moderate smoke conditions still existed in the structure. The crew began to look for their wayward brother.

While conducting their search for this "missing fire fighter", one member of the search party fell partially through the attic floor and ceiling below. After gathering his thoughts and composure, the fire fighter, with the aid of others, was pulling himself back up into the attic area when from below he heard someone shout "ARE YOU ALL RIGHT?" The firefighter looked down through the hole in the ceiling he had just created, and saw the image of the missing firefighter, in SCBA, full turnouts, (however bunker pants were at ankle length) sitting on a commode!

The fire fighter acknowledged that he was indeed uninjured from his near fall through the ceiling. He yelled down to his fellow fire fighter "WHAT THE HELL ARE YOU DOING?" To which the supposedly "missing fire fighter" replies; "What does it look I'm doing?'

After the fire on the upper floors was extinguished, this relieved fire fighter was assisting with overhaul in the ground floor business's, one of which was a beauty shop. The other utilities had been disconnected by fire fighters at the building, but the phone service was still working. Overhaul crews were ankle deep in water on the first floor and the phone was still ringing in the beauty shop. Word of the fire had traveled fast in this small town, and women were calling left and right to see if the beauty shop was still open.

Each time the phone in the nearly ruined beauty shop rang, this firefighter would answer it saying, "FIRE DEPARTMENT". This usually resulted in a hang-up on the other end. Finally one brave shaky voiced lady asked "Is the beauty shop open?' To which the fire fighter responded, "Define OPEN"

After a long shift and a very weird fire, the fire fighter finally returned home where he recounted his heroic deeds during this disastrous fire to his loving wife. Feeling sorry for him having missed sleep, and proud of his "heroic deeds", she made him a breakfast fit for a king. Afterward, she suggested he jump in the shower, and then extinguish her BURNING DESIRE.

As he rapidly pealed his clothes from his body, his wife exclaimed, "WHAT THE HELL HAVE YOU BEEN DOING?" To this he responded, "What do you mean?" She replied, "Look at your butt!" As he turned and looked in the bathroom mirror, there was a dark black soot ring around his butt where he had sat on the commode during the fire. Certainly a mark of honor for a job well done!

Chapter 2

"We found a young man sitting on the floor in a pair of bloody underpants, with a blood soaked towel in his lap"

THE CAB

Daniel Bryan

Brooklyn, NY

Dear Captain,

I am not a Fire fighter. I am waiting for my number to be called to go to the academy. I do have a good story for you. It's more of an observation I had while I was on a break at my job. I couldn't get the Truck number but it should be somewhat easy to track down because of the location if you decide to use this anecdote.

While on a break at work, I saw the damnedest thing I've ever seen. I have been waiting to be hired by the FDNY for a while, but if I hadn't been interested in the fire service before, this incident would have sold me on the profession.

I was taking a mental siesta and was staring out of a fourth floor window, facing the intersection of 42nd Street & 10th avenue. No thinking, just staring, watching the freaky and not so freaky people. I noticed up the block that a fire truck was waiting for the light at 43rd & 10th. When they got the green they made a very slow, very wide turn up on to 10th Avenue, then double parked the truck and put on the hazards. This caught my attention because they weren't using the red emergency lights, just the hazards.

I looked up and down the Avenue for the disaster. I had a perfect bird's eye view, but view or not, I couldn't find anything. No big pot hole, no broken down car, no fire in any of the apartments, hell... not even a jay walker. I continued to watch as everyone emptied out of the rig, save the driver, and started walking down 10th, against the traffic. They fire fighters crossed 43rd, and three of them walked up to a gentleman standing on the curb at the corner. A couple of the fire fighters broke off and started walking into the heavy, early morning traffic.

These two hailed, no... stopped, a cab coming up the avenue and MADE him pull over. All up and down the Avenue there were cars double parked, so the fire fighters were forced to hail the cab two lanes into traffic, not including the lane for parked cars as 10th is five to six lanes wide, depending on how you drive. This is New York after all.

Anyway, what was happening was that there was a blind man trying to hail a cab. No one was stopping and with 10th being the way it is, this guy was having a big problem. The fire crew saw this as they made their way down the street, and decided to help. They caught him a cab, literally, and helped him over. They didn't help him into the car, in fact they barely touched him as they escorted him over. They gave him the respect of a man, not a handicap or an invalid. This was the most powerful image I have ever seen.

I plan to see some serious fires in my career, and some scary times as well. I don't expect that that moment will ever be topped for me though. I apologize to the guys in the truck if this gets printed because they will probably just be embarrassed by this.

Take it or leave it. I think it's a great story. Good luck with the book.

Stay safe,

This is the greatest story sent to me. I think it speaks more about who fire fighters are then any other single tale in this book.

WASHING THE ENGINE
Fire Fighter Gerry Ashton
Hopewell Hose Co., East Fishkill, New York

Before I moved to Vermont, I was a volunteer firefighter with the Hopewell Hose Co. in East Fishkill, New York. The company took delivery of a brand new, Young Custom Pumper. Everyone was excited as this was the first new engine they had received in about 30 years!

Within the first week or two that the new pumper came on-line, the new car, I mean "new engine" smell still lingering, the crew rolled it out of the fire house to a report of a brush fire behind a home. The crew drove the engine into the yard behind the house to get to the fire, which the fire fighters quickly extinguished. With the fire extinguished and the lines picked up, the team mounted up and started to drive back around the house, heading for the Station. Unexpectedly, the engine fell through the ground and into a cesspool! So much for that new engine smell! In the end, the not so new rig had to be pulled up with a large commercial tow truck.

TOO YOUNG TO DIE

Captain Paul Youdelis - Station 12, C Platoon
Clark County Fire Department, Las Vegas, Nevada
I hated this call. This young man died, and shouldn't have.

This was early in my career. I was just a firefighter at the time. We were dispatched to a medical call for a man who had been injured when the crane he was operating tipped over. When the crane fell, The young man was thrown into the control levers of the machine, jabbing them violently into his abdomen.

On our arrival, the young man (I think I remember him being about 18) was laying on his back outside the crane. He was complaining that he couldn't breath. We started an assessment while waiting for the ambulance to arrive. He was completely stable with good pulse, blood pressure, and respirations. He was also completely alert and oriented, talking to us and answering our questions. His abdomen had some light bruises on it but he had no other complaints.

We finished our assessment, and put him on some oxygen. The ambulance had still not arrived, so I asked our Captain to get an ETA. Our dispatcher contacted the Ambulance company and advised us that the ambulance would be there in a minute or two. I continued to talk to the young man while waiting. We had been on scene now for around 8 minutes.

I noticed my patient was starting to get pale. We elevated his feet to help combat the effects of shock and I rechecked his pulse which felt a bit thin, and faster than it had been. I decided I should recheck his blood pressure. It had fallen a bit. I was becoming concerned. We had been on scene well over 12 minutes and still no ambulance. I asked the young man how he felt. His reply was slower, and less clear. Now I was really worried.

I asked Cap where the hell the ambulance was. Again he called for an ETA. The dispatcher came back and told us that the first Ambulance had gotten lost, and that they would send another unit.

One of our Fire Department ALS (Advanced Life Support) units became available, heard our calls over the radio and asked if we needed some help. I told Cap "hell Yes." By the time all of this happened we had been on scene with this poor guy for over 25 minutes. The patient was almost unconscious, I could feel no radial pulse and his blood pressure was in the toilet. He was dying. I have never felt so helpless.

Our ALS unit arrived shortly after hearing the call. We were loading the patient up in our Rescue as the ambulance arrived... over 30 minutes later.

The young mans heart stopped beating as he was being rolled into the emergency room. Despite the Doctors best efforts, they were unable to revive him. I can still feel the helplessness. I can still see this young mans life slipping away. I can't help but think of how things would have turned out if he had gotten to the hospital 15 minutes sooner. If he had gotten to the hospital when he should have. The answer will haunt me for the rest of my life.

TWO OF A KIND
Captain Tim Kjensted - Station 12, B Platoon
Clark County Fire Department, Las Vegas, Nevada

We were working a particularly hot, smoky fire. As we arrived, our company was assigned to do a life search. We entered the building and started crawling along, looking for anyone who might be in the building.

In the thick black smoke visibility was almost zero. I was crawling down what must have been a hallway when I bumped head first into another firefighter crawling in the other direction. I turned to move around him and he turned the same way at the same time. I made a move to go the other way, so did he.

I had crawled into a floor to ceiling mirror, and he was me.

PEPCON

Captain Paul Youdelis - Station 12, C Platoon
Clark County Fire Department, Las Vegas, Nevada

I was at my apartment where my fiancé and I lived. I was on the phone with her when we heard a series of fairly loud explosions. We both heard the booms even though we were many miles apart. Just as we started to discuss what the booms were, the big one hit. The Pacific Engineering Plant (PEPCON) blew itself off the face of the earth with the force of a small nuclear device. PEPCON was a plant, that specialized in a chemical called Ammonium Perchlorate. An oxidizer used in the manufacturing of rocket fuel.

A welder was making repairs at the plant and started a small fire. By the time he discovered the flames it was to late. Mixing an oxidizer with fire is like throwing gasoline into the blaze - times ten. 911 calls came in as workers in the plant started running out into the desert. One man, in a wheelchair, remained behind to call for help, and was lost in the tragedy.

A series of explosions began to rock the factory as workers fled. Next door sat the Kid Marshmallow Factory. The employees at Kid, now alerted to the impending disaster ran for their lives as well.

The final tremendous blast vaporized the PEPCON Plant and took out the neighboring Kid Marshmallow Factory. The concussion from the blast was felt throughout the Las Vegas Valley, shattering windows and cracking walls for miles around. Hundreds were hurt.

An engine from the Henderson Fire Department was approaching the scene when the final catastrophic blast hit. The shock wave blew the windshield from their engine into there faces, injuring the Captain and the Engineer. By the hand of God, only one person was killed in the blast

I remember deciding that I would head into the main fire station, knowing that a blast of that magnitude would require many hands. When I arrived, I was assigned to a reserve engine and sent to the scene. The landscape was like nothing I had ever seen before. We were shuttled into the area in a pick up truck. I felt as if I were on Mars. Shrapnel and debris were strewn about for miles in all directions. Smoke filled the sky, and the silence was creepy. The only sound I remember hearing was the sound of our Self Contained Breathing Apparatus (SCBA). We passed a rail road crossing. The gates had been thrown like tooth picks. Railroad tracks that ran to the plant were ripped up and bent like spaghetti. Abandoned cars were everywhere and were crumpled from the concussion. Their roofs were flattened by the force of the blast.

I spent almost 24 hours on the scene, operating amongst the rubble. I still can't believe that only one person lost their life. The bright spot of this tragedy for me was the time spent operating at the marshmallow factory, Molten marshmallow was everywhere. There was very literally a river of the melted marshmallows flowing out of the remains of the Kid plant. It was like a demented scene from the Willy Wonka movie. My turnout gear was covered in the sweet sticky goo, and had to be removed from service afterwards.

FORK YOU

Chief Gary McQueen
Sandy Fire District. # 72, Sandy, Oregon
Paul, I was reminded of a few other notable calls I've been on.

Several years ago, In Sandy Oregon, we received a report of a man that had been impaled with a pitchfork. These two brothers claimed that they were hauling a wheelbarrow load of yard debris down a hill, with the pitchfork on top of the load. The wheelbarrow hit something, causing the pitchfork to fly forward and impale the other brother in the neck.

I didn't believe the their story, as it happened too perfectly to be an accident. This man had a 4 tine pitchfork impaled, nearly to the hilt, in his neck. The 2 center tines were perfectly centered around his trachea. He was conscious and alert, but very frightened. There was no excessive blood loss, but he was somewhat shocky looking, (probably from fright).

Looking at the back of his neck, we could see that the skin was blanched from the ends of the tines nearly protruding. We activated Life Flight, based out of Portland, to get him quickly to a trauma center, besides we felt it would be a smoother ride than by ground. We decided that we had to remove the handle in order to transport him. So, we secured the handle with several hands and used a hack saw to gently cut it off. It worked well and we loaded him in the helicopter.

The story that I heard later was that after they arrived at the hospital, the flight crew was rolling him into the E.R. when an unknowing woman came walking around the corner and and came face to face with this horrific sight. She fainted and fell right to the floor.

FORK YOU, TOO
Name withheld

Our rescue crew was called to a report of a stabbing in a seedy part of our area.

The crew responded hot, and on arrival found the police already on the scene calling them in. The team grabbed their bags and headed on in. Inside they found a young black man with a fork stuck in his chest.

It seems that an argument ensued at the dinner table over the last chicken leg. The argument grew, quickly becoming physical when the victims brother snatched up a fork from the dinner table, plunging it into his brothers chest.

The kicker of the story is the comments made by the assailant as he was being lead out in handcuffs by the police officers. The EMS crew heard him say, "Give my my chicken leg. I fought for it, I won it, I'm gonna eat it!"

DEAD EYE DICK

Captain Paul Youdelis - Station 12, C Platoon
Clark County Fire Department, Las Vegas, Nevada

The call was for a shooting with no other information. Firefighters are brave soles but certainly not foolhardy. Calls like this, we hold back and wait for the Cops. The police live for pistol wielding fruitcakes, us... not so much. Officers arrived and cleared the apartment, then waved us in.

We grabbed our bags and headed into the apartment. There, we found a young man sitting on the floor in a pair of bloody underpants, with a blood soaked towel in his lap being held by his girlfriend who was kneeling beside him.

"What happened?" We asked. The young man stated that he had shot himself in the crotch. My partner and I exchanged agonized looks. We asked him "How bad was it?" and he replied, "I was afraid to look." We moved the towel and pulled back the bloody Fruit of the Looms to find a neat bullet hole in one side of his penis and straight out the other. He had shot a hole right through his wiener. The bullet went in one side at the middle of the shaft, out the other side at the middle as well, and finally lodged into his thigh.

The Young man had been planning to test for the Police department the following day and was playing it up for his girl friend. He had his loaded pistol stuck into his waist band, practicing quick draws when the weapon fired, piercing his man meat.

Considering the delicate nature of his injury, the fellow kept his sense of humor. We were preparing to start an IV with a 14 gauge needle to help replace fluids as he was bleeding pretty severely. A 14 gauge needle is kinda like a garden hose with a point on it. We prepared him for the impending IV stick by telling him that it would hurt. He said "It can't hurt any worse than this." gesturing towards his bloody crotch. As we stuck the very large needle into his arm, he said through gritted teeth..."I was wrong".

SOMETHING SMELLS LIKE SHIT
Fire Fighter Karl Lee - Station 23, A Platoon
Clark County Fire Department, Las Vegas, Nevada

We had been called for a teen girl who was having a seizure. I had already hit the rack for the night, and when the alarm came in, I just couldn't seem to get my head right.

When we arrived on the scene. I had sleep still in my eyes I couldn't even find the sidewalk, so I made a beeline for the house right through the front yard. Try as I might, I couldn't clear the halos from my eyes.

The girls father met us at the front door and led us through the house, to the girls room in the back. We found her in a confused, drowsy state that comes after a grand mall seizure. We started with our assessment, blood pressure, heart rate, respirations and such, when I turned and looked at the firefighter to my side....He smelled like shit!

It was just awful. I was trying to breath through my mouth with very little success. The smell was everywhere, but I didn't want to say anything out loud. I could see that the Captain could smell it too, from the rotten look on his face. Normally we might think the seizure patient had lost control of their bodily functions during the seizure, but it didn't seem so in this case. It had to be the other fire fighter.

He turned to put the stethoscope away and the look on his face clearly said that he could smell the shit, and he didn't do it. All we could think was that the girls Dad had ripped one. In the small unventilated room, the smell was almost more than I could bear.

What had happened was that I had stepped in a huge pile of dog loaf on the way through the front yard and had tracked the mess all the way through these folks house. The entire House reeked of crap.

Well, anyway, we all got a pretty good laugh out of it.

DRAGGING JIM BOB

Lieutenant Joel "Smoke" Feltner, CCEMT-P PROBOARD
Nuttall Vol. Fire Department, Lookout, West Virginia
Paul, here's a sort of scary call, but funny after the fact.

As the Lieutenant of a small town, rural fire department in southern West Virginia, we respond to many situations. One afternoon we were toned out to a possible structure fire 10 miles out and down a one lane country road. As always the directions were not the best so it took us some time to find the scene.

Upon arrival we found a small 5 room farmhouse that was abandoned and being used as a seasonal hunting camp with flames showing. It was off season at the time. We had to position our apparatus on top of a hill looking down at the house. To access the house we had to walk down the hill, crossing a three strand barb-wire fence on the way, then across a small flat and up another bank to the house.

The structure was 35 percent involved when we arrived. Myself , Jim Bob and one other firefighter started laying a 2 1/2 inch line down the hill and intended to wye it off into two, 1 3/4 inch attack lines. About 3/4 of the way down the hill, after crossing the fence we were at the same level as the house on the opposite bank. That's when all hell broke loose!

I noticed the distinctive sound of pressurized gas leaking. Suddenly the roof vented and shot flames in the air, too high to see. The sound was deafening. I turned, threw the 2 1/2 inch load that was on my shoulder down, grabbed Jim Bob,and started running back up the hill toward the trucks.

Now being a large guy (6' 2", 350 pounds), I'm not known for my speed, but am considered a pretty strong dude. I was running up the hill, through waist high weeds, dragging Jim Bob behind me. I didn't even slow down at the fence and ran right through it. When I heard the tell-tell sound of a freight train (which I have always been told meant it was going to BLEVE), I threw Jim Bob to the ground and jumped on him to cover him.

As I landed there was a loud "HUHHH!!" sound, which came from of course, Jim Bob. After a few seconds with no explosion coming, I jumped up, grabbed Jim Bob and raced back to the truck.

Arriving back to the Engine I turned around and found that the house had basically disintegrated. It wasn't until after we realized that everyone was ok that we all had a pretty good laugh. My Captain said that I looked like a 350 pound deer sprinting up the steep hill, dragging Jim Bob behind.

After making the 50 or so yards back down the hill and extinguishing the remains of the house, we found 3 large propane tanks inside. One had a large gash down the side, the other two were empty. This was one of my most memorable calls, and it scared me to death, but was funny all the while.

P.S. I have a lot more stories, both fire and EMS, if you would like to hear those too, e-mail your reply and I will send them. Thanks and be safe!

CHAPTER 3

"You could tell that she was in a state of despair. She was crying and saying that her baby was not breathing."

EASY RIDER
Chief Gary McQueen
Sandy Fire District. # 72, Sandy, Oregon

About 3 years ago, in Sandy, Oregon , we received a report of a motorcyclist that had gone over a cliff near the Sandy River. When I arrived, I was directed to the edge of a back yard. The victim had been riding a 3-wheeler around the yard and made too large of a circle. He got too close to the edge and just went right off!

I found a safe vantage point to see him and was amazed to find him nearly 130 feet down a sheer vertical drop. More amazing was that the patient was conscious! He was lying in a pile of soft dirt and rocks. We yelled to each other easily and I told him we'd be right down.

Initially, I wanted to rappel to him but we had had a very wet winter and the cliff face and landing were very soft dirt and limestone. Rappelling would endanger the victim and rescuers with falling debris.

The road to the house we were at continued down to the river, so we drove about one quarter of a mile down and guessed at a place to hike in. We got lucky with the location and had to hike in only a short way but it was in thick brush (Lesson learned? Carry machetes. We got some after this call). When we reached him he was in amazing shape. The only injuries he had were a minor one to his head and a dislocated shoulder. It took us another hour to get him packaged, hauled out, and in a helicopter on the way to the hospital.

Certainly, a higher power was looking after him that day. This guy should buy more lottery tickets!

DEATH

Garrick Parson

Paul, my name is Garrick and I've been in the fire service for 12 years. I have 2 stories for you. feel free to use them if want.

The first incident occurred in may of 1996. I was working full time with an ambulance service. We were toned out for a working structure fire about seven blocks from the hospital that we were based out of. While enroute we were notified that there was possible entrapment.

Just before our arrival we were told that there were positively two children trapped in the structure. Just as we pulled up, Fire Department personnel were bringing out the first child. She was 18 months old, was not breathing and was pulseless. CPR was started. I was just about to get out and transport the first child when I was met at the back of the rig by a firefighter with the second child.

CPR was also started on the second child who was only about 4 years old. we went ahead and transported both to the hospital, the rig packed with personnel trying to save the two children, Efforts at the hospital went on for over an hour, but in the end, CPR was called and both children were pronounced dead.

LIFE

Garrick Parson

The next story takes place in November of 1999. I'm a volunteer fire fighter here in my hometown. We were dispatched to a structure fire in our district. The call also came in as possible entrapment.

We were running hot when we were notified by one of our lieutenants that there was definitely someone trapped. Once we got there we climbed out of our engine. There was a lot of action everywhere. We were told that the child was in his bed room and we went in to search mode.

Myself and another fire fighter entered the apartment and did a quick primary search but were unable to find anyone. At that time we exited the room through the window we had originally used to enter. I reentered with another fire fighter to try again. Fire conditions were getting very bad by now and other crews were trying to use hand lines to cool the room down for us. We were in there about two minutes that seemed like an eternity, and we finally found the 4 year old at the foot of his bed. I handed him out the window to other fire fighters and bystanders. I came out next. It was very hot and I bailed in a hurry. While leaving I lost my boot, and much to my surprise my partner came out with it.

After my hurried exit, I looked up and saw the little boy lying on the side walk. I went over to check him out. He was breathing, very slowly. The Medics moved him to their gurney, we loaded him in the ambulance and they whisked him off to the hospital. The boy was taken to a major children's hospital in our area and to everyones surprise he was discharged 3-4 days later. He's doing fine now from what I have heard.

I hope these two stories will help you with your book. This shows the two different aspects of fire fighting. I enjoy this field very much.

Like I said, I hope this helps you. Let me know if I can be of any other help to you. Your brother in fire fighting.

SWINGERS
Chief Gary McQueen
Sandy Fire District. # 72, Sandy, Oregon

This happened just a few months ago. I was the duty Chief on this particular night. We got a report of a fire alarm at the local motel at about 2 a.m. A duty officer and engine responded, and I listened at home. After a few minutes of them arriving, they requested that I respond to help with the sprinkler system.

When I got there, the Captain met me at the door and he could hardly talk from trying not to laugh. A couple had checked in to a room and they brought a few things with them. A VCR, a porno tape, and of course, a "love swing".

This "Love Swing" thing hangs from the ceiling and - well I think you know the rest. The problem occurred when they were trying to decide where to hang the swing. It hangs from a chain with a small carabiner to attach, well, somewhere. So, guess where he tried to connect the carabiner? That's right, the sprinkler head. Only, the opening in the sprinkler head was smaller than that of the diameter of the carabiner. The anxious gentleman forced it a little, and proceeded to push out the fusible link and lever of the sprinkler head. Things then got a little wet.

When I arrived, there was about 2 feet of standing water in the room and hallway. Water was quickly spreading to the adjacent rooms. The sheet rock was coming down off the walls from the force of the water spray. All told, probably about $15,000 in damage to the building. The VCR, and TV were soaked and probably destroyed. The movie title? Something like... "The incredible squirting machine". No kidding.

Well, I appreciate the fact you are writing a book and I hope you get many responses. It doesn't take long in this profession to come up with some pretty amazing stuff. Good luck.

THE DEATH OF AN INNOCENT

Charlie

Paul you know as well as I do that sometimes firemen cry. even if it is on the inside. This is my story of the time I had to let it all go.

We responded to a call involving an infant not breathing. I was driving the fire truck that shift and as we arrived on scene this young mother came running out of the apartments. You could tell that she was in a state of despair. She was crying and shouting that her baby was not breathing.

We entered the apartment finding the father and a neighbor both frantic and over the baby. As I looked down at this pretty blue-eyed child I could see that he was not breathing. I started giving CPR at once. Nothing was going to keep me from saving this child's life.

As I started CPR I knew we had a great problem because the ambulance was at least 10 minutes away. I told my Captain we needed to transport the baby on the fire truck and that he would have to drive. We gathered the baby up and ran to the rig. The father of the child desperately wanted to go with us. This is something that we just don't normally do, let a civilian ride on a hot run. Anyway we just couldn't say no. we told him to get on, and hold on.

My captain was now my driver and he was hauling ass down the road just as fast as he could go. We hit a dip in the middle of the road and my head hit the the roof on the fire truck. I still kept on with CPR, nothing was gonna faze me. I just knew by then that the baby was dead but I kept on doing my job. As we arrived at the hospital I thought it was all for nothing, but I pushed on. I ran into the emergency room and hollered out that we had a code.

The nurses took the child from me at this time and rushed into a treatment room. My Captain was giving the report to the nurses and was going to ask me a question, but I had gone into the nurses lounge where it finally hit me. I cried and shook and everything else. Ugly crying. All of my emotions came to a head, it was very, very tough. The baby was about three months old. The same age as my child at home.

This was all I could think of. I could see that baby as my own. The captain finally found me in a clump on the floor crying uncontrollably. He new exactly what my thoughts were.

This happened over 15 years ago and I can still see the babies blue eyes. I can still smell the scent of him. After I had composed myself I went out of the lounge and a nurse came to talk to me to say I had done a good job. The baby had a pulse and was breathing on his own.

Then the emotions hit me again. They in fact just hit me again while I was typing this. I had to stop to wipe the tears from my eyes. We went back to the station and finished the shift with no other calls, thank heavens.

We called the emergency room the next shift and checked on the babies condition. Still no change, He was listed as guarded. The next shift we were on duty the parents came to the fire station to thank us for what we did for their family. They brought us some food and told us thank you.

The next day we called the hospital to check on the baby andwe found out that the baby had died. This was a great shock and let down for the whole crew. We cried for the family. All of us.

Our city fathers gave us a certificate of honor for doing our duty. This was kind of lame I thought, but we did give that mother and father a little more time with their baby. At that time on the fire department there was little known about critical stress incidents. I kept this inside me for about 8 years until I talked with our chaplain about this incident.

You know that firemen are supposed to be super macho. No feelings or anything of that nature. We have learned that that is not always how it happens. We have feelings and strong emotions. We now have trained people that are in place for critical stress. We have sent our people to other cities that have had some kind of incident that required this kind of help. We sent our Director of EMS to Jackson Mississippi when a fireman went on a shooting spree and killed four other fire officers. Hopefully, no more Emergency Personnel will have to carry their pain alone anymore.

Paul I know this is a long story but you asked for, now you have my story. I hope I can use my experience to help others if they need it. thanks for letting me tell one of my tales.

Charlie

Thank you for taking the time out to reply. Sending this painful memory Took a lot of courage. It will certainly help the folks who read my book see what firefighters are truly made of. I am a father of 4 and know where you are coming from. Just remember, When this child needed help, you Answered the call. Be proud. Someone, somewhere, knows this. Thanks for everything brother.

GO SHAVE YOUR ASS

Assistant Chief Joe Planck
Clark County Fire Department, Las Vegas, Nevada

My son is a firefighter for the same department I am. In a recent, harrowing, off duty, twist of life, he had a recent rectal cancer scare. He was scheduled to have an exam of his rectum and colon. Needless to say, he was more than a bit worried.

A fellow fire fighter from his station heard about his problem and had gone through the same thing himself. He had, in fact, had the very same examination that my son would soon be undergoing. He decided to give him a call the night before the procedure to calm any fears he might have.

He called over to the house and my sons wife answered the phone. He asked for my son, without identifying himself. She replied that he was not at home. He than said, jokingly, "I understand he will be having an anal probe tomorrow."

"Oh Doctor," She replied, not recognizing his voice. "I'm so glad you called. We have a few questions."

My sons friend, having had the very same procedure, decided...What the hell. Might as well answer a few questions and have a bit of fun at the same time.

My sons wife began asking questions, and he started answering them. At the end of the conversation the friend said that he had one last instruction. Trying his very best to not laugh as he said it, he told her that My Son would need to "Shave his anal region!"

My sons wife burst into laughter, as did the friend. Surly the jig was up. After the waves of laughter died down, my sons bride resumed the conversation saying "I'm sorry for laughing at you Doctor. But he is going to just hate this. I can't wait to tell him" The friend couldn't believe it! She still didn't know he wasn't the doctor!

A week later, after a successful procedure and no cancer (Thank God), word broke that my son not only shaved his anal region, he in fact shaved his entire ass, smooth as a babies bottom.

I guess a smooth rump is a small price to pay for a clean bill of health.

FLASHOVER
Captain Paul Youdelis - Station 12, C Platoon
Clark County Fire Department, Las Vegas, Nevada

I have been a firefighter for over thirty years. In that time I have been involved in many, hairy situations. Through all of those years, on all of those calls, I have never really been in fear of my life until I responded to this call.

We were called to a report of smoke in a home at a ritzy country club. We were the first unit on scene and found heavy smoke issuing from the hugh 4000+ square foot home and flames shooting from the attic vents.

I told my two fire fighters, Rik Leavitt and Dan Chapman, we would make a fast attack with an 1 3/4 inch line. the idea was to get a ground ladder up and get water into the attic trying to get the fire knocked down as quick as possible. My fire fighters pulled the line and got the ladder up, as other companies started to arrive.

We were making no headway with our initial efforts so me and my crew teamed up with the crew of Engine 18 to make an interior attack. We all masked up and made entry into the home through a side kitchen entrance. We found the staircase, and made our way upstairs where the fire must have been, only to find nothing but intense heat and smoke.

We needed to pull the ceiling and open some windows to vent the building. Try as we might, even with our longest pike pole, we couldn't reach the ceiling. We were also unable to locate any windows to vent the building. Our efforts in the building were proving futile, and the heat inside was building up to a dangerous level. I told Captain Paul Young from Engine 18, that we had better get the hell out of there.

As the words were coming out of my mouth, something behind me caught my attention. The entire room was lighting up! It was a flashover! I hit the deck as flames filled my face mask. I remember a total moment of clarity where I thought to myself "This is bad. This is very fucking bad." Fire fighters have to get to the seat of the fire to get it out, but being engulfed is outside the norm. I was shouting into my mobile radio that I had emergency traffic. I was calling out to abandon the building. Rik was using the line to try and keep an escape route open for us as we all hustled on our hands and knees to the staircase. I was still calling into my mobile to abandon as I fell halfway down the stairs.

We all got down the stairs and bailed out of the building. I ripped my mask from my face and did an immediate head count. Both Rik and Dan were Missing! That's when I really shit. After a quick check, we found that Dan and Rik had just used a different exit that took them out on the other side of the building. I breathed a hugh sigh of relief and passed command of the fire to another officer. I need to spend a little time over at rehab.

To this day, I know someone was looking out for me and my men. I was glad to get home the next morning to give my wife and kids a big hug.

DURRRR!
Battalion Chief Gary McQueen - B Shift
Lake Oswego Fire & Rescue, Oregon
Dear Paul, I got a cc of your request for stories from the job. I have a few.

Several years ago, I was an engineer on E-214 in Lake Oswego Oregon.

One night, Fire Fighter Dan Carpenter and I were sitting on the front bumper of the engine. It was a warm summer evening and a pretty young lady appeared on the sidewalk across the street.

While Dan was watching her, I stepped behind the overhead door of the next engine bay and let out the loudest DURRRR! sound that I could. It echoed off the walls and across the street. She looked straight over at the Fire Station and all she saw was poor Dan sitting there all alone, with his arms crossed. He just grinned, chuckled and said "Pretty good, Gary... pretty good". So much for our public image that night. I wonder what she was really thinking as she strolled along?.

THE CHEF
Fire Fighter Don Price - Station 12, C Platoon
Clark County Fire Department, Las Vegas, Nevada

We were called to a man with a knife in his abdomen, on the fabulous Las Vegas Strip in front of a popular casino. On our arrival, we were directed by Security to the edge of a planter where we found a gentleman, about 47 years old or so, holding a 15" chefs knife to his stomach. The disturbed look on the mans face told us all we needed to know. This wasn't a stabbing, it was a suicide attempt.

My Captain called for the Police to expedite, as we helped the security officers clear the area. The man didn't appear willing to talk, and we weren't about to get close to that knife. After all, Fire fighters aren't trained to disarm knife wielding folks intent on killing themselves. This was a job for the police.

Several Officers arrived on the scene, prepared for anything, a few of them with weapons drawn. The strip was shut down due to the crowd of gawkers flooding into the street angling for a better view. The officers were negotiating with the distraught man, reasoning with him, and trying to dissuade him from this drastic action. It was decided that they would try to wait him out.

As time passed, the gentleman had shoved the knife into his abdomen almost 2 inches, as the Police tried to stop him with their words. He was begging them to shoot him. The police didn't want to do anything to provoke the man, and they certainly didn't want to use lethal force, but they were prepared to prevent the man from leaving, even if they had to kill him.

Finally, there was a break. The police had convinced the man to talk to us about his medical situation. The Police Sergeant came over to our Captain and discussed their idea with him. The concept was for the "friendly fire fighters" to engage him in conversation and attempt to get him to let them near to check his medical condition.

This kind of thing is not what we normally do, but something needed to be done before the man pushed the knife further in, doing irreparable damage. Me, the Captain, and my partner Jim Ortiz, moved in to about six feet, eying the knife the whole way. Cap was talking to the man in soothing tones, telling him that we meant no harm, and asking him to move his hands away from the knife so we could help him. We were showing him the oxygen tank and mask, telling him that we were there only to help and that all we wanted to do was give him some oxygen, check his pulse, and blood pressure. We inched our way slowly closer as the man finally cracked, moved his hands away from the knife, allowing us to help him. We moved in. Cap and I took control of his arms while Jim took charge of his legs.

After we were done, and the man was loaded into the ambulance, Cap turned to me and said, "Were you nervous?"

"Nervous, hell!" I replied. "I was shaking like a leaf."

"Good," Cap said. "I'm glad I wasn't the only one."

THE DUI
Battalion Chief Vince Pirozzi
Carson City Fire Department, Carson City, Nevada

(St. Petersburg, Florida, August 1980)

In my 28 years in the fire service I have personally responded to over 12,000 calls. This one incident stands out in my mind as having the most affect on me, even to this day.

In August of 1980 I had about five years service as a firefighter / paramedic and was assigned for the last three to station #3. This was a small five man station in the heart of a ghetto area in the middle of the city that was also known as "The Knife and Gun Club". The station windows were all boarded up and we had 8 foot fences around the building to protect us. There were even bullet holes in the bay doors to make a point.

Besides the standard turnout gear, we were also issued bullet proof vests which we were required to wear when in this area. As a crew, we were very close, and practically family to each other. This was especially true for me and my regular partner. The station housed a three man engine company and an ALS rescue ambulance with two paramedics. As an average, we responded to over 15 calls per shift, with many days over twenty.

On this particular day, it was about 1400 hours and we already had had 6 or 7 calls, so we knew it was going to be a busy one. We had just backed in from the last call when the tones went off again for a pedestrian accident. As we headed out, the dispatcher relayed that it was a little girl and she was hurt real bad. I saw the look on my partner's face and I knew he was thinking the same thing as me. God how I hated calls involving kids!

It was about a four minute response, and just prior to our arrival the dispatcher informed us that police were on scene and the little girl was not breathing. As we arrived in front of the house there were a dozen or so frantic people who all seemed to rush at us before we could even get out of our rig. I had just put both feet on the street when a police officer ran up to me from the crowd and handed me the limp body of this little girl. I could tell immediately that she was a trauma code and there was no way we could work on her in the street. I jumped in the back of the ambulance with my partner and had the cop block the door because the people, some of whom were screaming in Spanish, were trying to get in with us.

An immediate assessment revealed that the girl had some serious head trauma and was indeed coded. My partner asked the officer if he would drive the rig to the hospital so we could work on her on the way. He jumped in the cab and away we went.

I had the head, so I was attempting to get an airway while my partner performed CPR. I remember looking into her eyes while I worked. She was a very pretty little girl with the biggest, darkest eyes that just stared wide open and lifeless into mine. We did everything we could during the short ride to the hospital and even had time to give a brief radio report to the awaiting staff.

When we arrived, they were waiting for us and immediately started working on her even as we wheeled her in. They must have spent at least a half hour and got the same results as we did. No response at all! I remember the emergency room doctor turning to me as I stood along side and he said: "What we have here is a dead little girl."

While my partner went to put our rig back together, I talked to the officer and asked him how the accident had happened. He told me that apparently the little girl was playing by the curb in her driveway when she was run over by a hit and run driver. The only information they had was a description of the vehicle as being a gray van. This information just made matters worse and at this point both my partner and I were very angry.

After we got our rig cleaned up and ready for service, we both knew that we needed to cool off and decided to just drive around for a while before going back to the Station. We took a ride for about a half hour and were venting our anger over what happened. I remember graphically describing what I would like to do to the low life that left the little girl to die in the street. My partner also made comments using some descriptive words that I am sure do not appear in any medical dictionary. It felt good to get it off our chests.

After a while we decided to go to the scene one more time before heading back, to see if they had anymore information on the hit and run driver. The area was roped off with tape and full of cops and they were interviewing the people present there. As we pulled up, an officer rushed over to us and said "boy am I glad to see you". Dispatch has been trying to get you for over 30 minutes, we even sent out a unit to look for you." When I asked what was going on, he said that we must have had an open mike on our radio because for the last half hour we had been broadcasting to the whole County about our plans for the driver. I immediately looked down at the radio and sure enough, the mic was squeezed between the seat and the console with the transmit button pushed in. We both knew we had some explaining to do to the Battalion Chief and our Company Officer. Needless to say, we headed back to our station for a certain chewing out.

As soon as we had the station in sight we could see the entire crew, the battalion chief, and what looked the fire chief himself standing in the driveway waiting for us. I immediately checked the mic before making a statement to my partner about what I thought would happen next. Our company officer came up to the rig and instead of chewing us out, he told us that he thought we would like to know they had caught the driver. This definitely was good news until he told us how the driver was caught. It was this bit of information that made it the most tragic and senseless incident that I have ever been unfortunate enough to be involved in.

It seems that just after we left the scene the second time, a gray van pulled up and drove through the barrier tape and up the driveway where the little girl was killed. The driver stepped out carrying a paper bag quickly tripping and falling. The bag broke and glass bottles of beer shattered on the ground. As police officers approached, the driver attempted to get up but could not because she was too intoxicated. She was the mother of the little girl and did not even know what was going on. After questioning she indicated that she had run out of beer and got in her van and backed out the driveway to go and buy some more. She evidently ran over her own daughter who was playing in the driveway and never even knew it until the police told her.

I never really found out what happened to her after that, but to this day every so often, I see those big round lifeless eyes staring back at me as if it had just happened yesterday. Oh, and by the way, except for a few snickers we never heard a word from anybody about our rather unauthorized radio broadcast.

A BOUNCING BABY

Captain Ed Rutherford
Roseville Fire Department, Roseville, California

When people ask me about my job as a fire fighter, they always want to know about the "stuff" I see on calls. I often think, "nothing really exciting in the last twenty five years." Sure would be nice if I could tell them that I saved a child from a two story burning inferno, but I guess its the small things that eventually add up to an interesting career.

There is one call that I seem to always remember. It happened back in 1975. I was working at the El Monte Fire Station, located on the edge of the Foothill Junior College campus in Los Altos Hills, California. The Fire Station is located just above Interstate 280, an eight lane split level freeway used for commuters going from the Silicon Valley to San Francisco. It truly was a high speed commuting freeway. Back in 1975 it only took about twenty minutes to get to San Jose. Now it takes twenty hours! Probably one of the reasons I left the department in 1982.

So, I have been in the business less than eighteen months and the bell goes off for a vehicle accident south bound 280. Heart bounding, I raced to my assigned position on the rig. I've got to laugh a bit at what we wore for safety gear back then. A well worn, used black turn out coat, no liner, hot as hell in the summer and cold and stiff as a board in the winter and a thin yellow plastic helmet with flip down "goggles". Cheap stuff but I wore that stuff with a lot of pride! That helmet still hangs in my garage.

Engine 73 and Squad 75 responded to the call. Engine 73 was staffed with one driver, by himself, while Squad 75 had two, myself and the Captain. "Squad 75, this is a single roll over in the north bound lanes."

All kinds of things start running through my head, "just don't screw-up in front of the captain!".

We arrived on scene. Cars are flying by, timing couldn't be worse, right during the commuter traffic. A light colored Chevy Impala convertible is upside down, flat, in the fast lane of oncoming traffic! I blindly follow Captain Baker towards the car, "Crawl under there and see if anybody is there." I didn't even flinch, I took off that plastic yellow helmet, and crawled under the car.

This young women was hanging upside down, It seemed the seat belt was holding her in. I said, "Are you all right?" Pretty stupid thing to say, but when you think about it, hell, I had never been to one of these before. I barely got the "all right" out of my mouth when the woman started screaming for her baby, "Where's my baby? Where's my baby?" Ice water ran through my veins. A baby! I saw the squashed car seat, but no baby! I looked back at the woman and she is no longer saying anything, I noticed her one arm hanging down. I don't think it was supposed to be bent in that many directions.

I quickly scoot back out from under the car, and head straight for Captain Baker to tell him about the missing baby! I could have been walking down the middle of the fast lane in on coming traffic and I wouldn't have noticed any cars racing bye, I was so tunnel visioned.

The 280 freeway was a split level freeway. South bound was higher, north bound was about eight to ten feet lower, separated by a dirt embankment. Captain Baker yells at me and another fireman "You and Phil go back up the embankment and look for the baby."

I don't remember how far back we went up the ice plant covered bank, but I just remember hearing Phil calling, "I found it!, I found it!" I kept thinking, this is not going to be pretty, I don't want to see this. Here comes Phil, he's got the baby in his arms, its crying like a pissed off attorney and not a scratch on it!

I don't even remember how old the little bugger was, but he was crying and that's all I cared about. The "old-timers' always told us, "as long as you hear the kids crying it can't be all that bad." Well this kid sure was crying!

We all headed back to the station. It was just another call to Captain Baker, but damn, I felt good. That woman seemed to just have a broken arm, minor bumps and cuts, but she had her baby, alive! It wasn't until about an hour or two later in the station that I realized I had witnessed a miracle.

I became very weak in the knees, lightheaded and I couldn't stop shaking. It is all I thought of for a couple days, it is something I'll never forget.

CHAPTER 4

"As I look toward the location of the call... my eyes light up. A large thick, black column of smoke could be seen rising over the trees near my house."

QUICKIES

Fire Fighter Ken Scofield, Ladder Company No. 1

Central Jackson Co. FPD, Kansas City, Missouri

Howdy!

My name is Ken Scofield, and I'm a Fire fighter on Ladder Company No. 1 with the Central Jackson County Fire Protection District in suburban Kansas City, Missouri. I've been in the fire service for just about 12 years now; for over 7 years I was a volunteer with the Camdenton, Missouri Fire Department, then I got hired by the St. Joseph Missouri Fire Department, spending 2 years there. I have been at CJC Fire for 2 & 1/2 years. Like most firemen, I too have a few stories that may help you out. Feel free to use them if you wish. Good luck on your project.

Ken Scofield

IAFF Local 3133

Firefighter, Ladder Company No. 1, C-Shift

Central Jackson Co. FPD

This is for all the EMS providers out there: We were dispatched on a 9-1-1 EMS call recently. The nature of the call: a mother called for an emergency ambulance because her 16 month old son was "experiencing difficulty having a bowel movement" When the radio finished blurting those words out, the firefighter across the table from me looked up at the speaker in the ceiling and asked, "No shit?"

****

Several years ago, I worked an accident where a patient was ejected. During the course of the ejection, this patient was also dismembered. I was assigned with a deputy to look for an arm. We found it. It had a Timex watch around the wrist, and it still worked. I looked at the deputy who said, "Takes a licking... and keeps on Ticking!"

****

I wasn't on this particular call, but know the involved crew well. There was a rollover accident in which a patient's ear became amputated. The patient was flown by air ambulance to a trauma center. The guys were asked to see if they could find the ear as soon as possible so a State Trooper could race it to the trauma center for possible reattachment. It was located between the window and the skin of the door; must have fallen in there during the impact. The guy who found it held it in his hands, close to his mouth and hollered, " HEY! HEY! CAN YOU HEAR ME!?!?"

THE TOY

Fire fighter Mike Gurr

Pompano Beach Fire Rescue, Florida

This story was when I worked with North Lauderdale F.D. , I now work for Pompano Beach Fire Rescue.. Thanks

Since I was born in Las Vegas (at Nellis Air Force Base) I will share this story with you.

We got a call for trouble breathing (SOB). I was on a Basic Life Support (first responder) engine company. We climbed a few flights of stairs, rushed in and found a young female wearing a baby doll teddy with some usless looking guy standing next to her.

The young lady appeared to be having some type of emotional crisis (crying). While we are assessing her, we kept on hearing a odd buzzing sound, or should I say a "vibrating" sound. Well, one of our guys (The class clown) decides to find out what the noise is. He reaches behind the bed & pulls out a 12 inch ADULT TOY!!

We fought to keep straight faces. As soon as we left we all broke down in laughter! I hope this is something you can use.

THE RAID

Fire Fighter Ken Scofield - Ladder Company No. 1
Central Jackson Co. FPD, Kansas City, Missouri

While I was working for the Camdenton, Missouri Fire Department, one of our Mutual Aid fire districts, Lake Ozark F.P.D., had just purchased a Sutphen 65 foot Mini-Tower. Since we were looking to replace our 1953 Seagrave 85 foot Ladder Truck, we paid close attention to Lake Ozark and their new purchase. They seemed very pleased with their truck. So pleased, in fact, that they recommended that we, at CFD also purchase one.

Their truck was impressive, especially when compared to our, shall we say, "classic" aerial. Theirs had a set-up time of less than a minute, meaning they could be going airborne and flowing water out the ladder pipe at the same time within a minute. Not our Blessed little Seagrave. We could throw the stick up just as fast, but then had to stretch hose up the ladder and hook it up the ladder pipe. That type of set up took at least four minutes.

Their truck was actually a quint, meaning it has a water pump, tank, ground ladders, and hoses in addition to the main ladder. The truck we would ultimately buy would also be a quint. Well, to make a long story short, we had ourselves become so impressed with their truck that we decided we wanted one as well.

Lake Ozark's personnel were very helpful, telling us how they thought their truck could be improved. They helped with developing the specifications for our truck and even came to Camdenton to put on a demonstration for our City Council. It impressed the Council so much that they were very enthusiastic about getting one for our town.

After a seemingly long time, our truck finally arrived. It differed a tad bit from Lake Ozarks, however. It came with a 70 foot ladder with one single platform and twin turrets. Naturally, a friendly rivalry developed between the two departments and trucks. On mutual aid calls, we worked well together. On mutual aid trainings, we would compete with each other. Who could set up faster, who could get the others wetter, and other such silly Reindeer games. You know... Hijinx.

Lake Ozark's mascot was the Tasmanian Devil cartoon character. The Taz! They have a stuffed Taz wearing a fire helmet on the dash of their quint. Our mascot is a fire fighting Bulldog. "The Big Dogs!" Not only did we have a stuffed bulldog wearing a fire helmet on our dash. We also have a Big Dog decal affixed to a 12 inch by 12 inch plate bolted onto the door of the basket on the aerial.

As luck would have it, somehow their Taz found it's way onto our dash! He was all tied up in Kurlex, with our Big Dog in a triumphant pose on top! We were proud as hell to have our kidnapped guest on the dash of our righ. Needless to say someone with ties to CFD happened to be in the Lake Ozark area on business... Our secret was out!

It took a few weeks, but finally the retribution came. I was in the stations office working on reports, and walked out to the bay to get a pop out of the machine. Something didn't seem right.... I didn't quite understand the feeling I had, but then it hit me...Wow! A blank spot on the basket door where our logo had been bolted and a bare spot on the dash with nothing left but an empty dog collar! SHIT!

That night was meeting night, and the fellas were starting to assemble. I announced to the membership that we had been dog-napped. Responses ranged from outrage to shock to disbelief to surprise! Eventually, a feeling that we got what was coming to us prevailed but, that didn't mean we would just take it! NO WAY! We take care of our own! The meeting was postponed and plans were immediately drawn up for a rescue operation.

We had several off duty sheriffs deputies in attendance, and the tactical training they received for drug raids and such was a huge help. We drew up a fairly detailed set of plans and set out to rescue our mascot

Dressed in full tactical clothing we synchronized our watches, armed ourselves with pressurized water extinguishers, dog biscuits, and set off on "Operation Mark Territory!!!"

We launched our attack with one group going to recover our dog.Heavy liquid combat ensued. It was complete mayhem. When Lake Ozark saw the going's on, they hi-tailed it out the door and armed themselves with the same ordinance we had, backed up with garden hoses and the booster line off a tanker!

Water and dog biscuits were flying about on what proved to be an ill timed attack. It would seem that we had a bit of a recon oversight. The Lake Ozark Fire Protection District Board of Directors were there having a Board Meeting. The Station was filled with Innocents! Opppps!

Please understand, those poor civilians had no prior knowledge of the friendly rivalry between our departments and had never seen firefighters at play. I wish we had a camera in the room. I would've loved to see their faces as all these commando-clad men came storming into their fire station.The Big Dog made it home and a truce was called. We even lent a hand in the clean up effort and shared a laugh!

A WELL DRESSED DEER
Fire Fighter John Hennessey
Turn of River Fire Department, Stamford, Connecticut
I am not sure how you would classify this story but it is true.

Our fire station backs up to the Merritt Parkway in Connecticut. One Fall evening an elderly woman walked into the firehouse to report an accident. This is not unusual because there is an exit ramp very close to the station and many people will drive by an accident then drop in and report the incident

This woman reported to the fire fighter on duty that she had just hit a deer on the parkway. This is also very common. She added that the deer was wearing a plaid shirt. This immediately got the alert fire fighters attention. He asked her where it, (the deer) was and the woman detailed the location.

The fire fighter immediately took the rescue up on the Parkway and found an man in a plaid shirt on the shoulder of the road. He had been hit by a car, but luckily not seriously injured. I'm not sure whatever happened to the woman or to the "deer".

HOT PUSSY

Explorer David Dragan

City of Knoxville Fire Department, Knoxville, Tennessee

My name is David Dragan. I am a Explorer with the City of Knoxville Fire Department located in Knoxville, Tennessee. I would like to maybe send you a little story or two about what we face over here in Tennessee as Explorers. I hope maybe this could shed some light on who we are and develop interest in the Fire Service.

My life as an explorer in the fire department has been very rewarding. Being only 17 years old it has been instrumental in my personal development and helped me make plans for my career. It has shown me a lot about the world and its interactions.

It was one of those days where I felt like nothing in the world could interrupt a day with the guys... Of course, my pager had it's own ideas and started beeping away. I immediately turned on my radio and heard several companies responding to a report of a apartment fire. I looked toward the location of the call and my eyes lit up. A large thick, black column of smoke could be seen rising over the trees near my house.

The incident was at least 15 miles away, so I knew this would be a good worker. My friends expressed an interest..so I told them to follow behind me and catch a glimpse of my favorite hobby. I jumped into my bunker pants, hopped into my car and raced to the scene. I arrived, grabbed my gear, and found the Incident Commander.

By this time, 2nd Alarm companies were arriving. I looked to the structure and the massive flames shooting from the roof. The Chief assigned me to my favorite Advisor, Earl. I assisted Earl with Rehab and looked for the arrival of the other Explorers. Once made it on scene, I set a channel to operate on and took Command of the group, assigning them as I was instructed by Earl.

Earls son Josh and I were assigned to an external attack along side of the regular firefighters. We were making good headway with an 1 3/4 line, when we both noticed a small animal crawl out onto a third story balcony and collapse. The animal was a small black cat that was reported missing to the chief several minutes prior.

We notified the chief. He sent Ladder 18's crew to try and help tha animal. We pitched in and helped them raise a 24 foot extension ladder up to the balcony. I took off my bunker coat to try and catch the cat as one of the firefighters went up the ladder to grab it. He snagged the feline and started down catching his boot on one of the rungs. He fell down slightly and dropped the cat which was caught be members below. They handed the cat off to me and Josh. At first, the animal seemed to have no pulse and clearly wasn't breathing. I quickly checked its mouth and gave it a few slight breaths and 5 CPR type compressions. I continued this Kitty resuscitation for about 2 minutes when the cat finally responded and started crying out and biting at us.

An EMT from the local Ambulance Company brought over an oxygen bottle and we tried giving the cat oxygen using a cannula and then a mask. The frantic animal bit into the mask getting its teeth stuck which actually ended up holding it in place.

The owner, relieved that her pet was alive, reached over to try and calm it. This was an epic fail. All she managed to do was further piss of an already pissed off cat. The Frightened kitty lunged out and nipped her hand tearing her skin and tissue deeply. After some time, the cat finally calmcd down enough for us to put it in a carrier and send it to an animal clinic.

The next several hours are really what can be expected at a working structure fire. We helped soak down the building, load hose, and take that 2 a.m. trip to the Waffle House to quell our hunger (The waitresses know us by first name already). This fire was a great learning experience for me, and brought me to realization of how much pets really mean to people. I felt as proud about our efforts to save this animal as if it had been a human, and still am.

CHRISTMAS SPIRIT

Assistant Chief Mike Forter
Lee Township Fire, Midland County, Michigan.

We responded as Basic Life Support (BLS) First Responders to a local tavern 2 days before Christmas. This Tavern is known for fights and arrests afterward. The call was for a Male, in his late 20's, that had been assaulted.

On our arrival, we found signs of the fight; the tables and chairs turned over and scattered about the room, glass broken on the floor, and three Police Officers doing their thing.

We interrupted their intense interrogation and started to treat the patient who had small cuts on his temple and nose. As we went about our business, we overheard the officers tell the remaining six (very intoxicated) patrons to leave.

The patrons were sloppy drunk, and they had all driven to the bar, so they couldn't leave without getting arrested for DUI, so they just stood around the bar, ignoring the order to leave.

We asked "what happened" to which our patient replied "I was assaulted with a deadly weapon" (Remember, this patient was VERY intoxicated). "What weapon was used" we asked. He replied "That chair over there, the dude hit me on the head with it!" (He had been hit LIGHTLY!, the chair was wood and hadn't even broken). We surveyed the patients head/neck area, and aside from minor cuts and a headache, he was fine.

About this time I noticed his sock, still on his foot, covered in blood. I asked "what happened to your foot foot?" "Well, the bastard hit me with the chair, knocked me down, and sat on my chest. I started screaming like a sissy from this awful pain in my foot. I looked down, I saw his girlfriend had pulled my boot off and was biting my foot!"

Silence ensued as we looked around at each other, trying not to laugh at this guy, when all of sudden we heard scraping and banging noises, accompanied by glass breaking and a lot of swearing coming from the corner of the bar. There stood the six drunks, unfazed by the mayhem, trying to right the Christmas tree that was toppled in the fight.

The tree, looking like a combat victim was halfheartedly leaning on one of the drunks, while the other 5 started to sing Christmas carols to it!! You've gotta love bar fights and drunks!

FASHION SENSE

Fire Fighter Sandra Bethge

Patchin Fire Hall, Boston, New York

Hello. My name is Sandra (Sandy) Bethge. I live in Boston, NY which is outside Buffalo. I do not know if this is what you're looking for but it happened to me and I'm still laughing today as I think back on it.

It all happened on a great spring day, I believe about 10 years ago. I was the first lady volunteer fire fighter in Patchin Fire hall and I was just out of basic training. Well it was just a matter of time, and then it finally happened... A car accident. My first call. My first chance to ride the engine. I rushed to the fire hall with my gear in my trunk and was the first to pull up to the station.

I started to jump into my gear while my husband (Also with the Department) and another fire fighter pulled the truck out of the bay. They were yelling "come on, lets roll." Well, in my hurry, I put on my bunkers not realizing my suspenders were crossed over the top of the pants. Mind you, all of my equipment was way too large anyhow, all mens sizes. I was swimming in this stuff! So here I am, running, or should I say waddling to the truck, carrying my helmet and coat, pants half up with the suspenders wedged between my legs! It must have been quite a sight! The Rig was about to leave as I tried to swing my half covered legs up onto the truck. All the guys were just rolling with laughter. I was so embarrassed. Well, I didn't let that call phase me and I stuck with it. I also learned a very valuable lesson! I learned to check my gear often and thoroughly after that!

FALLEN

Fire Fighter Isaac J Boehme

Munhall, Pennsylvania

My Brother,

My name is Isaac J. Boehme (Ike). I am A Volunteer Firefighter In Munhall Pennsylvania. I received an Email from you that was forwarded to me by numerous people, asking if anyone had any interesting stories From their dealings in the fire service. I do have one for you that is quite a tragic event that ends with a Line Of Duty Death of one the greatest men I have ever know. One whom I had known since childhood.

In August of 1995 I was only 19 years old and just beginning my life as a fire fighter. I was working a full time job and preparing to go back to High School to repair mistakes that I had made in the past.

On the Night of August 5, I had only been home from work for an hour or so before the tones went off and sirens started to wail. Before I knew it I was sprinting out the door and towards the station, which was only a few blocks away.

When I got to the fire house, I saw that the jump seats were filled with firefighters as the rig prepared to roll, and that I would have to jump onto the Tail board of our 1974 Mack CF600 Engine. I quickly donned my bunker gear (which paid off in the end) and jumped onto the tailboard with Bill (Spence) Marks . I was on the Drivers side and Spence, the passenger side.

We pulled out onto the front ramp and started our response. Everything seemed to be normal until re reached the crest of a steep hill. As we started down grade, the driver went to down shift the transmission but the manual transmission failed to cooperate and the engine came completely out of gear. The Engine lurched forward and started to careen down a steep, steep, hill from hell!

We were quickly picking up speed and it didn't take a brain surgeon to realize that we were in big, big trouble. The out of control fire engine first bounced off of two parked cars on my side of the vehicle. I horrified to see the 5 inch intake rip off of the pump panel and shoot by me. Next came the familiar "ting" of an Air Bottle hitting the ground. I glanced over my shoulder to see that one of our guys had jumped from the rig and was now writhing in the street in pain. It was at that moment I began to really fear for my life.

All blood drained from my face. I turned to look at my partner and could see the horror in his eyes - as if he knew he was going to be killed. It is a vision I can still remember very vividly, and do every single day. I braced my self as best as I could, pushing down with my feet and grabbing the hand rail in front of me with every ounce of strength I had.

The rig was a deadly meteor. We were catapulted across an embankment, and the engine rolled several times in a muddy area. My eyes slowly came open and I realized that I had been unconscious for a very short period of time. The first arriving rescue personnel came rushing down the hill to us. I remember seeing my friend and partner Spence hanging lifelessly over the ladder on the truck. I had to avert my eyes.

What followed can only be described as mass confusion. I could hear someone scream "He's in Cardiac arrest!" I instantly knew who they were talking about. It was Spence. I knew that I was in bad shape as well and couldn't even help my friend. My legs were numb and I couldn't breathe well. I found myself calling out for Spence. Imploring the growing throng of rescuers to save my friend I needed Spence to survive.

The rest of the event is now just a blur. I can remember being carried up the muddy embankment by numerous Firefighters. Most of whom were from the neighboring community of Homestead. Thank God for these folks. I will never forget them!

I was transported to Mercy Hospital of Pittsburgh and found myself next to the Friend I had know since childhood. The friend that I knew was dead. I didn't want to accept it. I think it was fitting however that I was the last person to be by his side both in life and then, after his death. This today is now a calming thought for me.

One of the medics who treated me that day is now my wife. I can go on and on about my experiences in the Intensive Care Unit and the memories I have of Spence and that night, but they somehow seem so distant now.

I hope this story may be of use to you. If you would like more please let me know. I am happy to help.

Sincerely and Fraternally;

Isaac (Ike) J. Boehme

IT'S OVER THE FENCE

Captain Edward McGrady, Jr.
Paterson fire Department, Paterson, New Jersey

I am a Fire Captain in the City of Paterson, NJ. I was assigned to Ladder Co. No. 3 on this soon to be, unusual night. We received a call to respond with Battalion 2 to River Street and 1st Avenue to assist the police department.

On our arrival, I called out on location along with the Battalion Chief. We could see a police cruiser on the scene and when the the officer noticed us, he came over and explained the situation. It seemed that an individual had tried to rob the house and while making good his escape he fell over the fence. When we went over to investigate we found the individual hanging upside down with his foot caught in a iron fence. Just hanging there. Upside down. The desire to laugh was almost overwhelming

The Battalion chief advised the individual that we were there to help him and to not bite or spit at us. I ordered my crew to get the little giant ladder. We placed it near him so he could climb up with his hands and take the weight off his leg. He cooperated and scrambled up the ladder with our help. We then turned him and his ankle so he could free himself. His freedom was short lived as he was promptly turned over to awaiting police officers for incarceration.

In my 17 years on the Department I have never seen a incident like this or as funny as this.

CHAPTER 5

"On the bed was a 73 year old man in t-shirt and his under wear which were quite disheveled. The patient was in full arrest."

FLICK YOUR BIC

Assistant Chief Mike Forter

Lee Township Fire, Midland County, Michigan.

We were at a neighboring department for a Fire Fighter I class, when the hosting department was toned out for a propane leak. Enroute, the dispatcher provided information that a lady had purchased a BIC lighter from the store, used it upon returning home and now the lighter would not shut off and was leaking gas.

The frantic woman placed the lighter on the counter, grabbed her cordless phone, evacuated herself, her son, and three cats from the house and called 911. When she called, she was frantic and positive that there was going to be an explosion.

Upon arrival, the three fire fighters found the lighter on the counter, with no remaining fuel, removed the lighter from the home and cleared. Upon returning to the station they were greeted by almost 50 volunteers from a Fire Fighter 1 class holding up lighters (lit of course) screaming "HELP ME, HELP ME!!!!"

NICE HOSE JOB
Fire Fighter Jason Neuman

We responded to a single family dwelling structure fire in my first in area. We arrived at the scene to find a single wide mobile home, heavily involved. I gave one of my "new" fire fighters the assignment to "Catch the hydrant and lay a supply line".

The Engine stopped, The young firefighter exited the rig and proceeded to the hose bed. For some reason it seemed to be taking an awful long time to deploy the line. I continued to look into the side view mirror for his signal to go and lay out the line. All the while I kept saying to myself "What the hell is taking so long?" Finally, we got the signal and laid out about 300 feet of four inch. I did a quick size up and had a pre-connect line pulled to attack the fire.

I hopped off the unit and walked past the back of the rig. My first reaction was..."What the @#%* is this?" Well, It seems that the rookie did get the 4 inch line but the reason it took so long was he also pulled a 2 1/2 inch line. Shortly after the fire was contained, the Chief walked up to my crew and said, "Now that's how you do it! Good job! You guys kicked ass." He turned to move on, walking past me. As he went, he slapped me on the back and said, "Excellent hose display!". Following in the footsteps of the Chief, the rest of the guys continued to pour salt in the wound with comments such as..."Nice hose job!", "What, 'you forgot which line to pull so you pulled them all?", and my personal favorite... "You sure do have a lot of hose on the ground there!"

After cleaning up from the fire, I had a post incident tailgate discussion with my new fire fighter. He quickly became an expert on a single forward lay.

RAGING RAPIDS
Battalion Chief Gary McQueen - B Shift
Lake Oswego Fire & Rescue, Oregon

Last January at about midnight, I responded with the Sandy Fire Department along with several other agencies to a Swift Water Rescue in the Mt. Hood National Forest. Two people were trapped on the roof of their car in the middle of a swollen mountain river. The air temperature was below freezing and the water was around 35 or 36 degrees.

We are fortunate to have a county wide, multi-jurisdictional team set up. We all get A-paged simultaneously, respond, and work as a team. This call stands out, as it was one of the scariest moments of my career.

We arrived after a 50 mile response, about 2 hours after the car went into the river. It was now around 01:30 hours. Sure enough, there was the car, in the middle of an 80 to 90 foot wide, very angry river. The water was high and flowing fast!

The Forest Service, a local rescue squad, and two of the other agencies on the team were on the scene when I arrived. The frozen, terrified victims were weakly calling for help. They were so cold it was clear they wouldn't be able to do anything to help themselves. They had almost stopped shivering. That's a pretty ominous sign of advancing hypothermia. We had to get to them before they began to lose consciousness.

Of all the people there, only 3 of us were qualified swimmers. Scott Walker, of Clackamas County Fire District #1, briefed me on his plan. Scott and I would walk up river about 500 feet and, one at a time, swim to the car. Each of us would then take off a victim by sliding a rope between the car and the shore, angled down stream. Don Maxwell, also from District #1, was designated as the "live bait" swimmer who would catch us downstream if something went wrong. Not a pleasant thought.

Scott jumped in the raging river and did a safety swim to the car. He easily climbed onto the roof and got both victims into a Personal Flotation Device. He attached the rope to a pillar of the car then took the first woman off the car. The car was rocking back and forth the whole time, but fortunately, remained in the same spot.

I waited out the minutes until Scott and the first victim reached safety and all of the downstream safety personnel were ready again. I took to the river, swam down to the car and ended up pulling myself onto the roof using the rope that Scott had set up. I noticed that the male victim only had his PFD clipped, not zipped so I tried to secure it when all of a sudden, the car jerked violently!. I shouted to the victim that if the car rolled over, to jump clear and I would get to him.

As soon as I uttered the words, then of course, it happened. The car violently began rolling over on to one side, and was starting to slip downstream. I yelled "JUMP!" and into the into the raging water we went, or so I thought. I desperately tried but couldn't grab him. Rather than jump clear, he kind of rode the roof of the car as it rolled until the car disappeared taking him under with it. When he didn't pop right up, All sorts of bad thoughts shot through my mind. I worried that his leg had become tangled in the rope or the car somehow.

finally, he corked up. I was being washed down stream, so I tried to swim against the current to catch him as he floated toward me. Don jumped in after us and we closed in on the victim in the middle of the river. The shore crew held their rope tight and at the end of the line we swung like a pendulum into the shore. The total time that I was in the water, on the car, and back in the water added up to only a few minutes, but they were a few minutes that will always fell like a lifetime to me.

A PAIN IN THE ASS
Assistant Chief Mike Forter
Lee Township Fire, Midland County, Michigan.

We responded to a home with an kind of apartment in the upper floor. It seems the young lady slipped on the wet steps while coming down the stairs, and fell hard, right on here rump. She was clearly in immense pain and we later learned she had in fact busted her tail-bone.

About one year later we again responded to that home, for a woman in pain from an unknown medical problem. We arrived to find the same woman with a beleaguered look, staring at her husband who was sitting at the dining room table, casually drinking a beer, "she's in there" was all he would say, pointing to the bedroom.

My partner and I walked in to find the same gal, lying nude on the bed, and again, in obvious pain. I asked what happened while my partner got a blanket to cover her (before others arrived to see exposed like this). "You remember me?" she asked. "I remember you, you helped me last time!!" I nodded, remembering her very well. After all, she was very attractive. "That son of a bitch in there! He went and bought this water bed yesterday. The doctor just told me I could resume my normal activities, and he just couldn't wait! He starts getting on me and all the while I'm telling him there wasn't enough water in the damn bed". She stopped for a breath, then said "He bastard just kept going!! Next thing I know, I heard something crack, then all this shooting pain!! He busted my damn tail-bone again!!!"

Sure enough, another busted tail-bone and another year of abstinence. We later learned that they got divorced!!!

JEFF'S FIRST FIRE CALL
Fire Fighter Jeff Kelley
Mahopac Volunteer Fire Department, New York

Friday, 15 January 1999

After being sworn in as a member of Truck Company #1 of the Mahopac Volunteer Fire Department on January 7th (I had to pledge to defend the constitutions of the U.S. and New York State to the best of my ability), I cooled my heels for a week, waiting to get my turnout gear and find out where my truck was and such.

The department canceled the regular Thursday training because of snow, still, there were a few folks hanging around, including the Chief and the Lieutenant of my Truck Company, Doug. Since there was time, Chief Smith and Doug fixed me up with some turnout gear. It turns out that probationary members get the important job of helping to make maximum use of recycled gear; my boots had 3 or 4 generations of firefighter's names on them and it took me over an hour to buff the visor on my helmet just so I could see murky shapes through it. Now of course, it's my favorite helmet!

Lieutenant Doug took the time to show me every item in every compartment of Truck #1. We spent a good hour going over all the equipment and talking about how it's used and such. I tried really hard to remember everything. I remember thinking that the jaws and their compressor were so heavy that I would need to spend some time in the gym, before I found myself having to carry the stuff up an icy embankment.

They didn't have a pager for me yet, but I had this old Radio Shack scanner at home, so I called up to get the frequencies and left the scanner on by my bedside and started doing what firefighters do best - wait.

I still hadn't had a chance to go on my first call and was scraping half an inch of ice off my windshield in preparation for going to work when my scanner played some tones I hadn't heard yet. Mahopac! "Downed Wires on Route 6 by Mahopac Supply!" There I am, all dressed with my windshield scraped and my engine warm and my little blue light just sitting there waiting to be tested. I'm Off!

I'm trying to race to the fire house only to get stuck behind some citizen who is driving his pickup at a snail's pace right down the middle of my street; oblivious (or maliciously aware) of my little blue light but I still manage to be the second responder to reach the firehouse. Everyone else is so calm. I half expected to be buffeted and shoved to the side I could almost hear someone saying "Hey Junior, why don't you just wait here and you can wash the truck when we come back?" I donned my turnout gear and was shown by the friendly Captain of Engine #1 where to park my butt on the jump seats behind the cab.

Great!. Doug didn't have a chance to show me where ANYTHING was on Engine #1. I can just hear it: "You, Kelley! Bring the 8-foot Cable Fend off Pole and a Number 3 Grounding Stanchion, On The Double!" Yikes! I told the guy next to me: "Hey, Brian, this is my first call, so if you want anything from me, you'll have to talk very slowly, ok?" He just smiled back and nodded understandingly.

The lights on the top of the cab were reflecting off the hose real and pump. Freezing rain was coming into our jump seats. All I could think is "How do they keep this thing so clean?" Downed wires. What did I read about that in the Brady Manual? All I could remember was something like staying more than a radius away from them. That's a big help.

We made a slow drive-by then stopped in the middle of Route 6. Someone in a pickup with a little blue light was talking to the Captain. The wires that are down looked a lot like cable TV wires. We started driving again and slowly cruise by Mahopac Supply, whip a U-Turn and then drive back to the firehouse.

We parked back in the station, with me having never even left my seat. I hopped off, and started to help wipe down the engine When the Captain walked by... "Hey, Cap, how'd I do on my first call?"

"Perfect, he said. Just perfect."

JEFF'S SECOND CALL
Fire Fighter Jeff Kelley
Mahopac Volunteer Fire Department, New York

Saturday, 30 January 1999

So I've got my kids for the weekend and we're sitting there watching a movie and my beeper goes off, "structure fire" in neighboring Mahopac Falls. I blurt "Gotta go" and I'm gone.

I made pretty good time getting down to the firehouse and jump on engine 18-4-1 and off we go to help Mahopac Falls. I'm in the cab behind the driver and we're running on red illumination (to preserve night vision). The six of us on the rig are all donning our turnout gear, bunker pants, helmets and Scott air packs in anticipation of the coming fight. As a probationary firefighter, I wasn't yet allowed interior so I wasn't donning an airpack. I was just trying to hold on to something during the hectic ride. The energy level was high since this sounded like a confirmed structure fire and not yet another false alarm.

We pull up alongside 3 other engines and trucks. There must have been 50 firefighters there and I could hear over the commotion someone say there was heavy fire venting from the windows. I craned my neck but couldn't see anything past the throng of firefighters. The Lieutenant says to me "Kelley, you're a Probie, so you'll stay with the truck; go sit up front with the driver and do whatever he says".

Eager to stay out of the way but get a better view, I climbed into the passenger seat just vacated by the Captain and sit there with my hands in my lap, thinking "don't touch anything, Jeff, don't touch anything!". All of a sudden, pandemonium breaks loose. There are sirens wailing just wailing away and air horns blaring! I'm looking around trying to figure out what the commotion is and realize that everyone is looking right at us! The driver shouts over to me "HEY PROBIE, GET OFF THE $&%*$# FOOT SWITCH!!!" I look down and realize that my jumbo fireman's boots are big-footing two ominous buttons on the floorboard.

After reflexivly yank my feet off the floor, get my flashlight out and read the signs on the buttons: Sure enough, they say "horn" and "siren". That figures! Shortly thereafter I was reassigned, and found myself standing in the rain a hundred yards down the road with flares and a flashlight in my hand, directing traffic, quietly wondering whatever happened to those siren pull cords you see hanging from the cab ceilings of fire trucks on TV.

Needless to say, my Probie gaff was the subject of some humorous comments and needling back at the firehouse. It seemed that everybody knew that Probie Kelley found the foot switches. I'm just hoping no one thinks of the name "Big Foot"; I've seen how nicknames come about and tend to stick in this business.

Did I mention? The movie I left my girls watching when I dashed out of the house? "Backdraft". No lie.

TOTAL SCUMBAGS

Fire Fighter Owen Hardy, Engine 1

Reno Fire Department, Reno, Nevada

Paul, I found your request for stories on the Firehouse web site. I work on Engine 1 in downtown Reno (hello from your brothers to the north, by the way I work for (Capt.) Mike Knapp who came to Reno FD from your FD or LVFD.)

This call occurred some months ago and came in as a stroke.

Engine 1 arrived at a rather seedy downtown hotel where we met with the ambulance who had also just arrived. A woman dressed in spandex tank top and some very short short-shorts met us and led us up to a room on the second floor.

As we entered the room we found two men just leaving the room whom we assumed to be helpful bystanders. On the bed was a 73 year old man in t-shirt and under wear which were quite disheveled. The patient was in full cardiac arrest.

We sprang into action and began to work him. As were doing our thing, we noticed that this was the girls room and quickly figured out that this man was her "customer." We managed to get a transportable rhythm so we loaded the patient on the gurney and got ready to roll. We helped get the patient down to the ambulance and two of us rode in with the ambulance to help continue ALS care.

The engine arrived to pick us up at the hospital. That's when we found out that the "bystanders" were actually the hooker's buddies and had not been helping the victim at all. They had rolled him, taking his car keys which they then used to steal a dying man's car!

Good luck with your book.

THE TRANCE

Lieutenant Robert Olson
Grand Chute Fire Department, Wisconsin

My name is Robert Olson, I work full-time as a Lieutenant for the Grand Chute Fire Department and am in charge of our EMS program. This was an actual call I ran while working Part-time for a private Ambulance Service in Waupaca Wisconsin.

My Partner Les James and I were dispatched by the Waupaca 911 center to respond in the county for a female patient with an unknown medical problem. Supposedly, the patient was possibly in a trance.

We ran code 3 to the area where my partner and I were met by a mid 40's gentleman who said his wife is in a trance. The man added that she wanted everyone to leave, and that unknown individuals were coming to kill her.

My partner and I staged in the driveway until the Waupaca County Sheriff's arrive and secure the scene. The officers entered, ensured that it was safe and then called us in.

My partner Les initiated contact with the oriental female who appeard to be in her mid to late thirties. She was sitting in the middle of the living room floor staring straight ahead. She became agitated by our attempts to assess her, and starts speaking angrily at us in a foreign language.

I asked the husband what the language was and he replied Chinese, she was from Taiwan. He stated his wife practiced Buddhism. The husband wanted his wife taken to a hospital for mental help but by Wisconsin Law the patient was able to make her own decisions and could refuse treatment, which she did.

Les and I played good EMT and bad EMT trying to convince this patient she needed help. We continued speaking with the husband who, through extensive interviewing stated his wife burned herself by sticking her hand in a bed of hot coals earlier in the day. That actually proved to save the day.

The deputy saw this as a threat of harm to herself and advised the husband he could and was going to put her in protective custody. We contacted our supervisor to brief him of the situation and he advised us to do what we had to. We contacted Medical Control who advised us that we should transport the patient to Steven's Point - St. Michael's Hospital for evaluation.

The Deputy attempted to place the patient into custody but she continued to sit in her trance. In the blink of an eye, she took off with all of us in hot pursuit, chasing her around and through the house. The Deputy managed to snag her and placed her in custody. He was moving her to the squad car for transport, but she managed to escape again and took off running through the front yard. She was again chased and wrestled with and finally put back into custody.

The Deputy secured her in his car and informed us he wanted us to evaluate her burn. It appeared to be a second degree burn and needed treatment, so as a team we placed the patient on our ambulance cot and secured her. We began the long, odd 27 mile transport to Steven's Point with her husband in tow to comfort his wife and provide her with a familiar face.

Once at St. Michael's the patient was evaluated by the psychiatric Doctor in the Emergency Room and we returned to Waupaca. with a heck of a story to tell

It seems the patient was in severe depression as a result of stress and it took almost 2 days until the hospital could find a practicing Buddhist to communicate with her and open the door for definitive care.

The moral of the story there is no such thing as a routine call.

Not the most exciting call to put on paper, but an experience of a lifetime.

Robert

CHICKEN

Investigator Jerry Sullivan
Rochester Fire Department, Rochester, New York

we were inspecting one afternoon, in an inner city neighborhood. The house was a 3 family frame structure. We got the key for the basement door from one of the tenants, and walked around to the back of the house to a walk-out basement door.

I had been at this house before, a year or 2 earlier so i knew my way. I unlocked the bilco door, opened it and stepped down to the basement door. As I was talking and opening the inside basement door, I heard a noise.

The door swung open and I looked up just in time to see three roosters fly into my face! Needless to say I was quite startled. Another way to say it is that I crapped my pants! I closed the door on the roosters, had a good laugh and decided that was enough for inspections that day.

LIKE FATHER, LIKE SON

Anonymous

Well I think I can help you with a short tale. My father has been a Captain for about 34 years on our local paid on call fire department. I've had family in the fire service for years. I've been a fire fighter myself now for about 5 years, with my local department.

I can remember my father coming home, tired, sweaty, and smelling like smoke. It just seemed natural that I would follow in his footsteps, and try to exceed what he had accomplished throughout his career. I'm hoping soon to take my test for State Certification as a Firefighter 2, and soon after that will be doing the same for fire fighter 3.

I've just become EMT and will soon be going to paramedic school. Its just funny how created and nurtured my longing to become a Firefighter I honestly love it!!!! I couldn't thank my Dad enough for showing me the best job in the world!!!!!

ROOM TEMPERATURE
Assistant Chief Joe Planck
Clark County Fire Department, Las Vegas, Nevada

In addition to our Engine, we had a Rescue unit at our station with two excellent paramedics Steve and Jim. On this particular shift, we had a brand new paramedic named Shaun riding along for training purposes.

The rescue received a call for a possible 419 (dead body). On arrival they found an older women who was obviously dead, but they checked her quickly anyhow to confirm that she was beyond help. Steve and Jim left Shaun with the deceased patient while they went to console her hysterical family. The pair had just gotten the family calmed down when they hear this shouting from the room where they left Shaun and the body.

"She's alive! She's alive!"

The family started yelling and crying in complete hysterics, while Steve and Jim rushed back to see what the hell was going on. They entered the room and Shaun yelled, "She's alive! touch her! She's still warm!"

What Shaun hadn't noticed was that the body was under an electric blanket. Shaun was promptly sent outside to wait for the coroner while Steve and Jim tried again to calm down the family.

CHAPTER 6

"The male resident is sitting on the couch, wearing nothing but a tee shirt with his johnson in his hand."

PENIS PROBLEMS
Investigator Jerry Sullivan
Rochester Fire Department, Rochester, New York
Ha! I got another story for you from Rochester New York.

Engine 5 rolled on an EMS run the night before last. They entered the house and walked into the living room to find the male resident sitting on the couch, wearing nothing but a tee shirt with his johnson in his hand. Everyone stopped dead in their tracks.

It would seem that his penis had some sort of "wound" on it and it was bleeding. I looked sort of like a big pimple or something. Needless to say, Engine 5's crew quickly turned the job over to the paramedics from the ambulance, who had just arrived.

RUNNING HOT. RUNNING REALLY HOT
Commissioner Rickey Brew
Islip Terrace Fire District, Long Island, New York
Does the attached count?

This is about a fire fighter competition which is fully sanctioned by our departments and as far as I know. This craziness is apparently only done by the volunteer departments in New York State. A crew of very insane fire fighters mount up on a special, seven hundred horsepower "Fire Response Vehicle", and race to see who can lay out from a fire hydrant the fastest.

All I can tell you is, no matter how many times you check the brakes, that one in a million failure of a $10.00 brake line can still rear its ugly head treating you to a hair raising experience! Nothing beats trying to dismount a 2000 lb. truck hauling ass down the track at eighty five miles an hour with the pedal dropped right to the floor by the driver. It's just plain nuts even if the brakes work perfectly!

On this particular run, We got to enjoy that one in a million failure and our team was literally flying with no brakes whatsoever, yet the two hydrant people still actually got off! I couldn't believe it! The Rig blew past the hydrant in the blink of an eye and the two were gone! Amazingly, they remained alive and were even still standing, but of course, running as fast as they could to stay upright. It was a hell of a sight to see.

YOU GO, WE GO

Fire fighter Jim Lee

Willow Grove Fire Company, Willow Grove, Pennsylvania

On December 20th, 1997 at 0234 hours, Box 35-71 was struck for 503 S. Warminster Road, at the Village Green Apartments.

The call was for a report of a fire in a building and the assignment called for Engine 10-2, Engine 10, Engine 95, Engine 15, Ladder 10, Ladder 90, and Rescue 353. In a matter of minutes, the responding units would hear reports that would certainly take things up a notch

"Chief 10, from County." Came the voice of the Dispatcher. "The caller in apartment T-5 states he is trapped in his apartment. The caller has dropped the phone. Unknown if he got out. We do have an open phone line." As the information came down, everyones adrenaline went through the roof. The dispatcher came back on a few moments later, "Assistant 10-1, Montgomery PD is on scene, confirming we have a working fire with people trapped."

On my arrival, I sized up the scene. We had a 3 story garden style apartment building with heavy smoke showing. As I walked up the driveway of the complex, I could see two people hanging out of a window on the left side of the building. I also noticed that the fire had a very large jump on us and had already extended into the cock loft of the building.

I called for a second alarm only ten minutes after the initial call. When I got around to the front of the building, police officers there told me that there may be more people trapped then the two at the front. Engine 95 and Ladder 10 were arriving. Ladder 10 was directed to throw a 28 foot ground ladder to the second floor and rescue the two trapped people at the front while the crew of Engine 95 pulled lines to attack the blaze.

Myself, Chief Steve Avato, and Fire fighter Jon DiLenno entered the structure and made our way to the upper floors. We reached the landing and saw no fire in the hallway, but flaming brands were raining down on us from the ceiling. The fire was running rampant in the attic. We started to search apartments, but could not get to the two end units because the fire had by now engulfed the rear unit on the left. Flames were blowing out of the apartment, preventing us from continuing the search, fortunatly, Engine 10 came up behind us and hit the fire with an attack line and cut a path for us into the adjacent apartment.

Fire fighter DiLenno and myself forced open the door of the apartment and started to search the last uninvolved unit. We had covered half of the apartment when we heard a rumbling sound come from the doorway. It sounded like a freight train had just crashed into the building. I whipped around to see the door we had come in was filled with fire and was ripping into the apartment. We were trapped.

The noise was the roof of the building collapsing just outside of the apartment we were in . When the roof came in, it dropped right on top of the Crew from Engine 10 and cut off our escape. Conditions in the apartment worsened and we found ourselves with only two options left... Jump 30 feet to the ground or try to head out through the engulfed doorway and hope for the best.

Outside of the apartment, things were just as bad. Sergeant Gershanick from Engine 10 took a direct hit from the falling roof. The other members from Engine 10 shook off the collapse and furiously dug Gershanick out from the burning rubble and removed him to safety. He sustained burns to his legs, but survived the collapse.

There we were still, trapped in the apartment forced to deal with our own situation. None of the truck companies had had a chance to throw up ladders to the rear windows where we found ourselves trapped and 30 feet was a long way down, so we opted to go back out the doorway we came in and hoped for the best. We both ran back out through the doorway and through the wall of fire, hoping for the best, not knowing if we would die before clearing the fire. We hauled ass through hell until we practically trampled Engine 10's crew. I will never forget what I saw when we got clear.

While one member of Engine 10's crew was dragging Sergeant Gershanick to safety, the rest stood their ground in the most hellish conditions with Chief Strange leading the attack. They were standing their ground, fighting to either get to us or at least offer us a way out! They were still there, because we were still there! They had been caught in a collapse, had a man down, had only one small attack line, and yet had no intentions of leaving without us.

After getting us out, it was decided that we would evacuate the building and have to go defensive. The building was too far gone. Thanks to the men Of Engine 10, I survived and made it out with only third degree burns to my wrists. The crews of Engine 10 and Ladder 10 went above and beyond the call of duty that day. They stayed until everyone was clear making a truly heroic stand... if you ask me...

THE WASHDOWN
Captain Lonnie Walch - Station 21, C Platoon
Clark County Fire Department, Las Vegas, Nevada

We got a call on I-15 toward the California State line, and if I remember it right, it came in as a washdown. When we got there, we found out it was in fact an Auto/Ped with the auto being a tractor trailer rig.

I-15 had earlier been shutdown for a police situation. It seems a man in a convertible was driving along, pointing a gun at people. Traffic was backed up for miles and in frustration this lady in an old beat up car gets into the emergency lane and starts passing everyone. A Highway Patrolman saw her, stopped her, and directed her pull to the shoulder and wait just like everyone else.

As the woman moved over to the side of the road, of course her car stalled. The officer had gone back to the original scene and soon after, traffic was allowed to flow again. The backed up vehicles started to un-bunch and the highway started to clear only to back up again near the woman with the stalled car. The frustrated officer goes back by to the spot where he left the woman and her car only to find that she had gotten out of her stalled car and had been hit by a Semi.

The truck driver said the victim was on her hands and knees in his lane and he had no chance of missing her. Looking at the deceased woman, you could imagine how the big rig had hit her. The bumper probably caught her about half way up her nose because everything above that was gone. All that remained was the bottom half of her nose, mouth and chin which appeared almost unscratched.

Her body must have been run over by the trucks trailer tires because her torso was mangled and twisted beyond recognition. We found brain and skull fragments hundreds of feet away. I remember thinking, how among all that mangled flesh, the unscratched bottom half of her face looked so out of place. The mess was so bad, the call did turn out to be a wash down.

GRAVY
Captain Jim Perkins, Station 21, C Platoon
Clark County Fire Department, Las Vegas, Nevada

I joined the fire department in November of 1970. When I came on, I was about the third on our hire list. I was told there was going to be a rookie school starting before mine but they asked me to come right on the floor as they needed someone immediately available to cover for someone who had quit.

I showed up all by my lonesome to work on the floor while there was this 42 man rookie school in progress. I was more or less given a uniform and set of turnouts. We didn't have SCBA's in those days, so I was given turnouts and was told if the alarm goes off, get on the tailboard and do what the other fireman does. The other Fire Fighter, Alan Stump, was my training. Strictly OJT.

Alan showed me how to put the turnouts on and while the truck had a couple of SCBA's on it, no one ever wore them of course... it wouldn't be macho to do such a thing as that.

I had been on only about three months. We were sitting down one afternoon to a dinner of fried chicken, a dinner that had always been considered a taboo on our department, because every time we ate fried chicken, we would usually get a big fire. Of course, just as we were sitting down to dinner when the alarms went off.

I was at old Station 18, on Desert Inn Road by the Convention Center. We responded to reports of smoke coming out of the eighth and ninth floor of the Regency Towers. The Regency Towers are about fifteen stories high and sit right in the middle of the Desert Inn Golf Course, it was a very exclusive, high rise condominium type building.

On arrival, Stump and I went to the elevator. I guess we were assigned to what now would be considered fire attack. Our Captain told us to go to the fire floor and find out what the deal was.

We went up to the 8th floor in the elevators, dressed in our turnouts - of course with no SCBA's. We didn't use high rise packs at that time and relied on the house lines. If there was a big problem, we could bring additional lines in to supplement the installed lines. Alan told me, "Normally we would use the stairs, but since this is on the eighth floor, were gonna go up in the elevator." He told me it was probably nothing. Just a pot on the stove or something like that. So don't worry too much about it. When we get out of the elevator just do what I do.

The elevator opened up on the eighth floor and to my dismay, it was pitch black. I couldn't see a thing through all of the thick black smoke. The building had a corridor that went around the outer side of the building. This outer corridor was separated from the outside with floor to ceiling plate glass windows and the inner side was bordered by walls and doors.

We got low and crawled out of the elevator. I went to the right, which would put me on the exterior side against the windows. Alan crossed over and went along the inside of the corridor by the walls. Alan called to me and told me to come over to the other side and to stay with him.

There was a lot of thick smoke and it was getting blacker and heavier. I started to wonder what the hell I was doing there. I didn't know a damn thing! We were down on the floor crawling with our left shoulders against the wall to guide us. The fire, we found out later had started on the eighth floor, and lapped up to the ninth. We actually had two floors that were pretty much fully involved, but at that time, we didn't really realize it.

We were crawling on the floor and this fire was rolling over us on the ceiling. It was just a big mass of, not really flames like you would see coming out of a campfire, but more like thunderheads. It looked like flaming clouds rolling down this hallway. I remember looking up at it, and thinking... "This is the coolest thing I have ever seen!" We got to the house lines, and started putting water on the fire. We could feel water hitting us from the other direction, so we knew there was another crew up there.

Anyway, it was quite an extended operation, probably four or five hours before we got the fire completely out. We had everything cleared out and had worked our way up to the ninth floor. We came back down and headed back to the elevator where we had originally gotten out and I was shocked by what I saw! I could see the floor to ceiling plate glass window where I had started to head, was completely broken out. If I had put my shoulder against the wall and started going, I would have fallen right out of the building, eight stories straight down.

It was a very good lesson to learn on my first fire, and I was relieved I didn't have to die to learn it. It was quite a dramatic first fire. Whatever made us switch over and put our left shoulder on the wall instead of our right saved me. I know it wasn't really Alan Stump's intelligence or leadership abilities. I can say that now since he's retired and gone (LOL!). But whatever it was, when I saw that window gone, my knees get all jelly like. I did know one thing from that moment on... I loved fighting fire. It's the gravy of the job. I loved EMS too, and became a paramedic, but fighting a working fire is still the gravy of the fire department.

TOILET SEAT SIZE-UP

Ex-Chief Robert R. Davis

East Bangor Volunteer Fire Company, Bangor, Pennsylvania

Here's my favorite "war story".

Several years ago when I was Chief of the East Bangor Volunteer Fire Company in Pennsylvania we had a call at about 02:00 for a kitchen fire in a single family home. The fire appeared to be minor and my guys did a good job confining it to the kitchen, or so I thought.

It would seem that when I'm awakened at 02:00, about 20 minutes later my bowel also awakens. Since the fire was out (we thought), I decided to "use" a bathroom located near the kitchen. As I was sitting there I heard crackling noises in the wall. The sound of fire! I yelled through the door to get a line into the attic as soon as possible.

The crew got up there just as the attic flashed over, but hit it hard and fast and saved the home. I call this "My toilet seat size-up".

OVERDOSED

Lieutenant/Dispatcher Chris Turrentine
I know its nothing very spectacular, I find it kind of bizarre though.

One evening around 17:30 I was on my way to my full time job as a 911 dispatcher when I stopped by the fire station to pick up something that I had left there the day before. When I got there, our engine and first responder vehicle were out on calls and the ladder truck was in the shop, so the apparatus bay was empty.

I grabbed my stuff and made a quick phone call. As I got off of the phone a car pulled up to the bay and a man got out exclaiming that he had an emergency. I was thinking he was going to tell me there was a wreck down the street as most people usually do. I started the man at his car and noticed that he and another gentleman started pulling someone out of the back seat.

The man they produced looked very bad, so I told them to leave him there and I would be right back. I went into the supply room to call dispatch and request an ambulance. I got off of the phone, got a pair of medical gloves and went out to help the man. As I came out of the supply room, I found the man lying in the middle of the bay with his friends and their car conspicuously gone. I ran outside the bay to see the car pulling away. I yelled for them to come back but they just waved and sped off.

I went back to the man lying on the floor and saw that he was not breathing and was blue from the nipples up. I was swearing up a blue streak I was so mad and frustrated. I ran back into the supply room and called dispatch and told them I had CPR in progress and quickly hung up.

I went to the medical supply cabinet and grabbed a bag valve mask then rushed back to the man. I checked for a pulse and found nothing. I then reconfirmed that he was not breathing. I guess I was nervous because I had never initiated CPR before and wanted to make sure it was really needed before crushing this mans chest.

I started doing compression's and after about 7 or 8 he attempted to breathe. He was breathing maybe once every 30 seconds, so I continued CPR, alternating between compressions and bagging him. The next thing I knew, our squad, truck, Engine, 2 ambulances, 2 EMS supervisors, 3 sheriffs officers, and a State Trooper arrived. I had never been so glad in my life to see...well... everyone!

The paramedics took over and before they departed the scene with the patient, he had a pulse and was breathing on his own. A few days later, he actually walked out of the hospital, fortunate to be alive. It seems an overdose had brought about his near demise. His "Good Friends" dumped him with me and took off to avoid some uncomfortable questions.

I just thought I would share this with you. Maybe you can use it in your book. Well, good luck.

THE BIG ONE
Captain Lonnie Walch - Station 21, C Platoon
Clark County Fire Department, Las Vegas, Nevada

We worked a code inside a camp trailer at an R.V. park. The victim was a man in his late sixties or older. His wife was there and about the same age. We didn't know for sure what caused him to have the "Big One", but it might have had something to do with the hugh Kielbasa Sausage laying in the sink with a French Tickler on it.

STUCK

Retired - Jim Benvenuti
Glenview Fire Department, Glenview, Illinois

I worked for the Chicago suburb of Glenview, Illinois for over 25 years.

One of the funniest calls I responded to was on a warm summer Saturday. We were toned out to respond to a home where a woman had her hand caught in a toilet.

It seems her 3 year old dropped his toothbrush in the toilet and when his Mom tried to remove it, her wrist became caught between the toothbrush and lower half of the toilet bowl. We tried pouring lubricant into the toilet to free her wrist to no avail. We could not see the toothbrush at all to try to reach it with a cutting tool. Nothing we tried seemed to have a chance to work.

We ended up unbolting the toilet from the floor and carrying her and the toilet out to the yard. Now this was a beautiful day and all the neighbors were outside enjoying it. As her neighbors watched we took out our trusty sledge hammer and carefully broke the toilet away from her arm until she was free!!!

BOOTS & COOTS

Tom La Sure

Hi Paul,

How about the story of a refinery fire in Artesia New Mexico at the Navaho Refinery?

This fire involved two 1,000,000 gallon gasoline tanks. We had every fire department for miles around on scene including Red Adair's people as well as Boots and Coots. We didn't have enough AFFF on scene to put the fire out and we desperately needed to get more. The call went out and soon we had foam arriving in car trunks, pick-up's, and on semi-trailer. finally it was decided that we had enough to fight the fire.

It ended up that the Incident commander was from Boots & Coots... The IC get's up in a room full of Fire Chiefs and big wigs and says "OK Men, here's the plan... We apply water to the rim of the fire for 15 minutes to cool down the fire, (1,000,000 gallons of gasoline are blazing away mind you) then we'll apply foam for 15 minutes to extinguish the fire!"

Way, way past the proposed 30 minute mark, the fire was still raging. TWO HOURS into the foam application we heard a rumbling, kind of like a thunder noise. Not sure what the hell was going on, we start looking around. All the local fire fighters were gone! That can't be a good sign! All that remained was their nozzles, in fact, no one was anywhere to be seen except my company! Well. The rumbling got louder and you could feel the noise building in your guts. Oddly, as quick as it started it, went away. Fortunately for us, what we didn't know was that earlier in the day, when there was still only one tank burning, the noise we heard was the same noise that came just before the tank blew up and started the second one on fire.

We were so very lucky that it didn't happen again. Needless to say the whole fire took almost 22 hours to extinguish.

this was the readers digest version I can stretch it out more with more detail about human chains to keep the trucks full of foam, the trouble we had keeping the Engines cool with that much fire heating the air near by, and so forth. Good luck!

CHRISTMAS DAY
Fire fighter Richard Okrasinski
SouthSide Fire Company, Owege, New York
I hope that this helps you out.

My name is Richard Okrasinski and I am a firefighter/EMT in the SouthSide Fire Company, Owego, NY. We cover about 62 square miles of mostly farms and residential areas. Our medical response consists of a converted bread truck with mutual aid for ambulance service. I have been with the department since 1992. However, since 1994 I have been on the inactive roster due to serving in the United States Navy, stationed in Bangor, Washington.

On shipboard, I am a Fire control Technician, whose job it is to track other ships and sink them when needed. I am also an EMT on board and have worked with the Base Ambulance service.

During Christmas holidays this year, I went back to Owego on leave. It was Christmas Day and we were relaxing while we waited for the whole family to arrive. Before my grandparents showed up, Owego was dispatched to a "Man who needed assistance getting back in bed." My Father (the Chief of the Company), my Sister (a Captain), an Assistant Squad Captain, and I all responded. It had been a while since I had made a run, so I asked if I could run this call since I was a little rusty.

The call was supposed to be easy. A lift assist. The Department had been called here before for this same type of thing. The patient was an elderly man who had Do Not Resuscitate Orders (DNR) and was confined to the bed.

We arrived on scene and were met by the mans son who told us his father was in the bedroom. I walked to the bedroom with my father and sister where we found the gentleman with his wife by his side trying to tend to him. He was in his 80's and not fully dressed. He had sat up then fallen out of bed onto the floor.

My sister left the room out of decency as he wasn't fully clothed while my father and I went to work. 2 more firefighters came in and we collectively prepared to move him back to his bed. I told him what we were going to do. His only reply was to blink his eyes. He said nothing to us. Before we could pick him up, we had to remove his tangled nasal cannula. We turned him around, so his head was on the right end and then moved him back into the bed. As we got him comfortable and restored the oxygen, one of the guys asked if we should take vitals and fill out the paper work. I decided that we should since it seemed very possible that we could be back to see him later in the day. He really didn't look very good.

His wife had told us she didn't expect him to make it past New Years, and I wanted to make sure our visit and care was documented. I reached down to take his pulse on the right radial... it was 92 and thready. My father on the other side, took the left radial but couldn't find it. He reached up and took the carotid, and still couldn't find it. As I leaned over to check his breathing, I didn't feel, see, or hear anything. I took a stethoscope and listened to the chest. No breath sounds, but a heart beat. I told my father this while he kept looking for the pulse. With his head propped up on the pillow, we figured we might have blocked his airway. We removed a pillow and rechecked his breathing. Still nothing.

The wife walked over and quietly asked "You can tell me, is he going to make it? His mother died on Christmas day, and he said he wouldn't let that happen to him. Is he going to make it?" My father looked at her, and in his best Chief voice said, "We really aren't trained to make those decisions."

My father was called by the dispatcher on the radio and left the room leaving the Assistant Chief and me in the room. I rechecked his pulse. It was now gone. I knew it was there a minute ago, so I listened to his heart. Thump-Thump, Thump...silence. His heart had stopped as I listened. I checked his pulse one last time, hoping that maybe I had just gone deaf. The Assistant Chief asked me for a heart rate, I just looked up at the man's wife. She went blurry as my eyes filled with tears. I said, "I'm sorry, there is no pulse".

I left the room, walked past my father and out to the front porch where my sister was standing with some other members. My sister saw me first and asked what was going on. I just looked at her and broke out into a full cry. She gave me a hug as I composed myself. I went back into the room where the Assistant Chief was standing there, just looking at the man who just five short minutes ago had been alive.

About a week later, the funeral came around, and I had returned to Washington. The obituary said, "all donations are to be made to the South Side Fire Company." Being my first call in a long time, this was one I truly learned from. No matter how hard you try, you will never save everyone. And the worst sound in the world, is the sound of a silent heart.

CHAPTER 7

"I looked in the street and I could see big splotches of blood all over. I saw the trailer. I could see the blood that had run down from the windows from where she had tried to smash the windows to get to her children."

MIA, ALYSSA, and RAIN
Captain Paul Youdelis - Station 12, C Platoon
Clark County Fire Department, Las Vegas, Nevada

It was an amazing Las Vegas evening. My wife and I were going to go to a Local High School to watch our daughter, a Cheer Leader cheer. We decided it was so nice out that we would take my wife's convertible.

We rolled out and turned onto the main drag of our little community, only to make it a couple blocks. As we approacehed the crosswalk that leads from the homes to the park, we saw cars stopping, and maneuvering about. My wife turned to me and said, "This doesn't look good." Boy was she right.

I maneuvered around some of the stopped cars to the area of the problem. I assumed there had been a car accident, and intended to see if I was needed to help. That's when I saw the tiny flip flops laying in the crosswalk. I just remember muttering "Oh, fuck me."

I got out of the car, told my wife to call 911 and to then move the car out of the way. I then rushed over to help. It was clear to me at this point that this was a an Auto/Ped. I still had no idea just how bad this night was about the be.

I pulled my badge and forced my way through the ring of mortified bystanders, announcing that I was a Fire Captain and to let me through. I was shocked to see not one, but three mangled little girls.

I shook the shock off and began assessing each girl. All appeared to be about 5 or 6 years old and all in critical condition. I ordered everyone not helping to back off, and asked if anyone had any EMS experience. I got nothing back except blank looks. I was gonna be going this alone.

I took those willing, and began to try and treat the girls. One was alert, one was balled up face down with blood streaming from her head. The third appeared to be breathing agonally and had a mangled leg shaped like an S. I directed helpers how to maintain C spine on the two girls who were on their backs. With the help of another volunteer, we were able to log roll the third girl and get her C-Spine protected. She was unconscious and I could find no pulse.

After getting them positioned we started to address airways. I couldn't be in two places at once, so I chose the pulseless girl to work with as her down time was only mere seconds. I could verbally direct the helpers with the remaining girls. I quickly explaind to my corps of volunteers how to try and keep their charge's airway open and tried to focus on CPR on my patient. At some point, someone from one of the local ambulance companies arrived and jumped into the fray. "Thank God!" I thought.

As I began CPR, the first Fire Department units from the North Las Vegas Fire Department began to arrive. I gave them a quick rundown and was so grateful that they were there now AND with a full complement of ALS gear. The Ambulance Company arrived soon after and between them and Fire they were able to throw and go with the two most critical patients. I was now free to move over to the third girl.

I began to care for the last girl until another Ambulance arrived. I handed her off and she was whisked away to the Trauma Center, leaving me wanting to collapse in relief. Frantic relatives were flocking to the scene, shouting and yelling so tried to help by calming them and organizing them so they could get to the Trauma Center as quickly and safely as possible. As the left, my immediate roll ended, but not so the Story.

****

These girls were a part of my wife's and I's lives now. We followed the news closely for any updates. Mia, Died a few days after the accident. The entire community was saddened by this tragic accident in so many ways. An Elderly woman unfamiliar to the area failed to stop at the cross walk and hit the three girls. Rain, suffered a fractured skull but recovered fully. Alyssa, the true miracle was transported to the hospital and was listed in very critical condition. In my opinion, she had almost no chance for survival, but after extensive time in a coma, Alyssa regained consciousness surprising everyone who was praying for her.

Today, Aylssa has made an amazing recovery. While she still has hurdles in her way, she is home, back in school and even running on the leg that had been so badly mangled. Aylssa is an amazing, precocious little girl with a bright future.

For my wife and I, we are torn. My wife Reggi, not being used to scenes like this will carry this with her for the rest of her life and will always mourn Mia. I too will forever remember that night and always pray for Mia. Alyssa is our bright spot however. Knowing that she beat all odds and is living a fruitful life helps us when we lament that night.

I'VE FALLEN, AND CAN'T GET UP
Captain Mark W. Gay
York Beach Fire Department, York Beach, Maine.

This is the scariest incident I have ever been involved with in my fire service career of 27 years. I joined as a volunteer in September of 1972 and was hired full time in June of 1983 to work a 24/48 shift

On a February morning in 1990 at 03:44 I was on duty at the York Beach Main Volunteer Fire Department. We received a call for a residential structure fire about 2 miles from the station. This fire was reported by Douglas Bracy, a Patrol Sergeant with the York Police Department while he was on his way home. Doug is also a volunteer member of the fire department and a friend of mine since our school days.

When we arrived at the scene, the fire had already vented through the front door and was burning up to the roof line of a 2 story wood frame building. Initially, the fire was darkend down from the outside then entry to the building was made through the front door. I was backing up the firefighter on the nozzel on the first line inside. I had only taken a step or two inside the door and fell right through the floor down into the four or five foot deep cellar. As I fell, I must have taken out some electrical lines, because all hell was breaking loose with electrical arching going on right beside me. There was a local couple video taping the incident and they saw an arc follow the lines down the pole to the ground. In the video you can see the arcing going on through the small cellar window.

When I went through the floor I landed on my feet with my head poking out just above the floor level as the cellar was so short. There was a Police Sergeant standing right outside the door when I went through and my partner on the line was just in front of me. They grabbed my arms and were pulling so hard I thought they were going to pull my arms out of their sockets.

It's amazing what goes through your mind when something like this happens. I had just married a wonderful girl and we were expecting our first child together. I had already had a son and so did she I could see their faces. With all the arcing going on I figured the fall didn't kill me, but electrocution would get the job done, and I would never get a chance to see my soon to arrive daughter.

The two were pulling on me to get me out but my airpacks regulator would catch on the shattered flooring. I finally got their attention and let them know that it was ok to let go of me. A chunk of the flooring was removed and with that gone, they were finally able to help me out.

Finally free of the hole I was whisked off to the York Hospital despite me best efforts to let everyone know I was fine. I lost that battle, as the Chief wanted me to go in and get checked. What the Chief wants, the Chief gets. When I arrived at the hospital the E.R. doctor asked me why I was there and all I could think to say was, "Good question".

ELIZABETH

Assistant Chief Joe Planck
Clark County Fire Department, Las Vegas, Nevada

I had been promoted to Assistant Chief and had only been in that position for a Month when the call I will never forget came in.

It was about 07:30 in the morning. I had just walked into my office when my pager went off. The dispatch came in... "fire in a mobile home with possible victims trapped".

Our Public Information Officer (PIO) had just gotten to work so we responded together. We got in his car and were faced with a long response across the Valley. I switched to channel 3 to monitor the radio traffic and the dire reports started to come in.

The first in Engine arrived on scene and reported the mobile home was fully engulfed in flames. As we continued to fight traffic it came across there were possibly three young boys, (three brothers, five, four and three years old), possibly trapped inside. I can remember as we weaved our way through the traffic praying that they were able to get the boys out. I felt almost desperate. The reports continued.

The first report came that the fire had been knocked down. Then I heard that they had found one victim. He was 419 (deceased). I can clearly remember my thoughts... I was praying to God, "please let them find at least one of them alive. At least one alive." Then the next report came in... they had found the second victim. He was also dead. At that point I knew that there was just no way that they were going to find the other boy alive.

As we fought our way through traffic, I was extremely frustrated. I can remember that tears were in my eyes. The thought of those three boys and the tragic way they passed as well as thoughts of what the parents must be going through. I was really frustrated because of the traffic. It seemed that cars were refusing to get out of our way.

When we finally arrived on scene the first thing I saw was a young mother sitting in the back of an ambulance, holding an 18 month old boy with her arms bandaged from the elbows to the wrists. I looked in the street and I could see big splotches of blood. I could see the trailer. I could see the blood that had run down the outside of the home from the broken windows, where she had tried to smash them to get to her children.

I walked over to the first in Engine Company. Mike Herrera, a young fireman who had been on only about three years was standing there. He had a dazed look in his eyes. When he saw me he started to cry. I walked to him and he threw his arms around me an just sobbed. He said "Chief... We just couldn't save them. We tried so hard. We just couldn't save them." The other firefighters came over and joined us in the middle of the street. I hugged them, and I tried to comfort them, but there was nothing I could say. Nothing could make this better.

The News Media started to arrive and the firefighters started bringing out the the boys in body bags. It's a memory that I will never forget. The memory of the three lives that were lost that day. The memory of three young children. I knew all to well that pain... I had felt that pain before. The pain of not being able to save a child, but had never had to deal with three at one time.

I talked to the firemen and told them, that my best advice was to go back to the station and then go home for the rest of the shift and just try to relax. I was being interviewed by all the different news media when one of our guys came walking out of the trailer. He had a big stack of photographs which was just a soggy mess, and was burnt around the edges. He said "Chief, we have got to try and save some of these". I took the pictures to a young girl, who was standing across the street and I gave them to her. I thought she might know a bit more about the family and what pictures might be important. She was glad to help.

After it was all over, we quietly drove back to the station. I had been in my office for about two hours when I received a phone call from one of the local news anchors and he says "I'm getting people calling in here. Somebody really needs to talk to them." I said "Well, there really isn't much we can do." He replied "No... You don't understand. People are wanting to donate huge, big things. Somebody really needs to talk to them." So I gave him permission to use my name and refer everybody to me at the station.

The next day when I came in, the receptionist was fielding literally thousands of phone calls. Every twenty or thirty minutes she had to be relieved because she just couldn't take it anymore. She was also a mother of 4. She had tears streaming from her eyes as she took the calls.

On the very first day we had offers of two mobile homes that were being donated. Two local mortuaries called and donated the services. A local casket company wanted to provide the caskets, and money from everybody, everywhere started to pour in. We had previously set up the Clark County Fire Fighters Burn Fund to assist fire victims, so we started to direct the funds through the burn fund. We found out the boys Father had left their Mom and she had been supporting the boys on her own, working in the kitchen at Caesars Palace. We received a call from Caesars. They wanted me to tell her to take six months off... with pay! Caesars was also willing put her up in a suite at the hotel as were several other properties.

The response from the Las Vegas community was overwhelming. I had to try and focus on the best things for Elizabeth. Out of the three mobile homes that were donated I had to choose the best one for her. It was a brand new one donated by the mobile home association. The other two were several years old. Walker Furniture donated a house full of furniture.

I had to organize guys to go around to the local fire stations to pick up the clothing and food donations that were being dropped off in mass. We got a storage shed on each side of town to hold donations, and soon those were full. I had spoken with Elizabeth. She was just overwhelmed with all of this support. She was a very gracious young woman. I sat and looked at the stitches on both of her arms, it was all I could do to even talk to her as I could feel her pain. It was just overwhelming.

I went to the services for the boys and a young girl came over and handed me a photo album. This was the same young girl I had given the pictures to the day of the fire. She had taken the pictures and cleaned them up, trimmed off the burned edges, and put them neatly into an album. I had the honor to present that to Elizabeth the day she buried her three boys.

THANKSGIVING

Fire Fighter Dean

Baltimore City Fire Department, Baltimore, Maryland

Dear Sir,

I am a Paramedic/Firefighter Apprentice with the Baltimore City Fire Department.Here is a story that occurred this past winter on Thanksgiving morning.

My partner and I received a call for an assault case which was right down the street from a station that housed a truck company who were assigned to the call with us. Because of the nature of the call, the Police Department was dispatched as well. The truck company was so close, they arrived on the scene within moments.

We arrived and maneuvered into a location behind the ladder truck and a police car. We grabbed our equipment and proceeded to walk to where the patient was. We walked into an abandoned

lot filled with old construction equipment and tank trailers that bordered some railroad tracks. The ground was mostly made up of crushed and broken bricks, making footing very difficult.

Our patient was a female in her early thirties. She was found half naked and barely breathing. She had a massive open head injury with exposed brain matter. She was breathing on her own but had severe airway compromise due to blood and teeth in her mouth. Right next to the patient's head, I was able to see what could cause such a horrific injury to a human being: there was a rock somewhat larger than a basketball stained with blood.

We focused on the critically injured patient, treated her expeditiously at the scene with IV's and supplemental oxygen via bag-valve mask. I shall never forget the feeling of the victims face as it would "sink" into her head while I tried to ventilate her on the way to the Shock Trauma Center. She clung to life for several hours, but eventually succumbed to her injuries.

Happy Thanksgiving!!

Please contact me if I can assist you any further or if you require any more information. Good luck with your "project".Thank your for the opportunity to share this story!

THE LITTLEST FIRE FIGHTER
Unknown

The 26-year-old mother stared down at her son who was dying of leukemia. Although her heart was filled with sadness, she also had a strong feeling of determination. Like any parent she wanted her son to grow up and fulfill all his dreams. Now that was no longer possible. The leukemia would see to that.

She still wanted her son's dreams to come true. She took her son's hand and asked, "Billy, did you ever think about what you wanted to be once you grew up? Did you ever dream and wish what you would do with your life?"

"Mommy, I always wanted to be a fireman when I grew up."

Mom smiled back and said, "Let's see if we can make your wish come true."

Later that day she went to her local fire department in Phoenix, Arizona, where she met Fireman Bob, who had a heart as big as Phoenix. She explained her son's final wish and asked if it might be possible to give her six-year-old son a ride around the block on a fire engine. Fireman Bob said, "Look, we can do better than that. If you'll have your son ready at seven o'clock Wednesday morning, we'll make him an honorary fireman for the whole day. He can come down to the fire station, eat with us, go

out on all the fire calls, the whole nine yards! And if you'll give us his sizes, we'll get a real fire uniform for him, with a real fire hat - not a toy one - with the emblem of the Phoenix Fire Department on it, a yellow slicker like we wear and rubber boots. They're all manufactured right here in Phoenix, so we can get them fast."

Three days later Fireman Bob picked up Billy, dressed him in his fire uniform and escorted him from his hospital bed to the waiting hook and ladder truck. Billy got to sit on the back of the truck and help steer it back to the fire station. He was in heaven.

There were three fire calls in Phoenix that day and Billy got to go out on all three calls. He rode in the different fire engines, the paramedic's van and even the fire chief's car. He was also video taped for the local news program.

Having his dream come true, with all the love and attention that was lavished upon him, so deeply touched Billy that he lived three months longer than any doctor thought possible.

One night all of his vital signs began to drop dramatically and the head nurse, who believed in the hospice concept that no one should die alone, began to call the family members to the hospital. Then she remembered the day Billy had spent as a fireman, so she called the Fire Chief and asked if it would be possible to send a fireman in uniform to the hospital to be with Billy as he made his transition. The chief replied, " We can do better than that. We'll be there in five minutes. Will you please do me a favor? When you hear the sirens screaming and see the lights flashing, will you announce over the PA system that there is not a fire?" It's just the fire department coming to see one of it's finest members one more time. And will you open the window to his room? Thanks."

About five minutes later a hook and ladder truck arrived at the hospital, extended its ladder up to Billy's third floor open window and 16 firefighters climbed up the ladder into Billy's room. With his mother's permission, they hugged him and held him and told him how much they loved him.

With his dying breath, Billy looked up at the fire chief and said, "Chief, am I really a fireman now?

"Billy, you are," the chief said.

With those words, Billy smiled and closed his eyes one last time.

People sure can be nice to people at times. God bless those firemen.

This was sent to me as a reply to one of my E-Mail messages. I don't know if it's true or what, but it brought a tear to my eye so I included it. To me, it speaks about all of the "Billies" out the who Fire Fighters help everyday.

ALL IN A DAY'S WORK
Fire fighter Jimmie Coiner
Chesapeake Fire Department, Chesapeake, Virginia

As a professional firefighter for the City of Chesapeake, Virginia I get to see many strange and unusual events take place. This one particular event happened at a local Senior Citizens Home.

We were dispatched to a possible head injury from a fall involving an elderly male at the home. Per our local protocol we sent an Engine with 3 personnel and a Medic with 2 personnel. When we arrived at the scene we found an elderly man in his seventies with a bleeding wound on his head.

The elderly man had no intentions of letting anyone get near him to check him out. He was attempting to hit, kick, or spit on anyone who approached him. All the while he was yelling something that we could not understand and then it finally dawned on me what it was. The man, who was retired from the military, was yelling for a field doctor!

I am not even sure where it came from but I caught myself yelling "Sergeant" and to my surprise, as well as everyone else's, the man snapped to attention and saluted yelling back at me "Yes Sir". I then said "Lay down and let that Corpsman take a look at you" which again to our surprise he did.

The Medic crew was then able to look at his wound, bandage it and transport him to the hospital without any further argument. I guess watching old war movies can help sometimes.

THE RECTAL EXAM
Battalion Chief Gary McQueen - B Shift
Lake Oswego Fire & Rescue, Oregon

We had a call for a man with chest pains one morning. After our arrival we placed him on oxygen, hooked him up to the Lifepak, and I began prepping for an I.V.

As I readied my equipment and snapped on a pair of rubber gloves. He said, "Son, if you think you're gonna stick your finger up my ass, you got another thought comin"!

MORE QUICKIES

Captain Paul Youdelis, Station 12, C Platoon
　Clark County Fire Department, Las Vegas, Nevada

I remember doing CPR on an infant who had been involved in a car wreck. No big deal. Just doing my job. I held this baby in my arms, doing the compressions, giving mouth to mouth. I had to do it. No time to think about it. Just move. I jumped into the back of the Ambulance with the lifeless infant in my arms, and we were rushed off to the hospital.

We arrived at the hospital, and the baby was whisked away from me. The Admitting Nurse came to me and told me I needed to go to the restroom and wash up. I walked in and looked at my face in the mirror. I had the babies blood all over my face. I was horrified. I saw my bloody face in the mirror and I knew. I knew that the baby wasn't going to make it.

I started to cry.

****

We had this fire knocked down. It was still hot and smoky in the house, and we needed to do a primary life search. I was crawling down a hallway to the back of the house where the bedrooms were located. I was feeling my way along the wall when I heard a eerie wailing coming from one of the bedrooms. A victim!

I crawled faster, following they agonized cry. I turned into the room where the sound was coming from. There was no victim. Just a smoke detector. Still in its box. Sitting on a nightstand with a battery in it. It was burnt and melted, but it still tried its best to call out its warning.

****

We got a call to respond to a Lava Flow in the middle of Las Vegas. Needless to say, we were unable to locate anything.

CHAPTER 8

"there were eight to ten people there and there was a couple with their arms around each other. They were all right in front of the elevator doors. They were all very dead."

THE MGM

A small fire started in a pie cabinet at the MGM Grand Hotel. The small fire worked its way unseen through concealed spaces, feeding on any fuel it could find - Growing.

It was early. Many of the Hotel Guest were still in their rooms, resting up for another big day in Vegas. Others were already in the Casino pulling the arm of their favorite slot machine. By the time the fire came out of hiding and the alarm was sounded, it was already too late. The MGM Hotel was doomed.

The fire that had been growing in the concealed spaces of the deli for some time finally showed itself. The Clark County Fire Department was called. Station 11 sat about 100 yards across the street and was one of the first units dispatched. They were on scene in nothing flat. On arrival the crew made their way into the Hotel. From the doors, all they could see was some smoke hanging at the ceiling level at the other end of the casino floor. They started their way back through the casino past the hard core slot players only to make it about halfway in.

A hugh fireball engulfed the far end of the building and was ripping through the Casino at breakneck speeds. The fire fighters turned and ran for their lives. They cleared the doors they had come in as the wall of fire flew out after them. This fire, one of the single worst fires in the Nations history, claimed the lives of eighty four people.

****

Battalion Chief R. B. Taylor - Station 18, C Platoon
    Clark County Fire Department, Las Vegas, Nevada

11-21-80, Friday THE MGM FIRE

Today is a day I will remember for the rest of my life. I know there will never be another day like it. Today the fabulous MGM Grand Hotel burned.

8:00 a.m. - I took a book up to Sandi at the bus stop. I noticed a large black column of smoke. I thought that it must be a tire fire or possibly a drill fire at the airport.

8:30 a.m. - I received a call from Dorothy informing me that the MGM Casino was fully involved. I could hardly believe it. I tried to call the Fire Department Dispatcher, but of course all the lines were jammed. We turned on the television and saw the news coverage on the fire. All off duty fire fighters were asked to report for duty.

9:00 a.m. - Bill dropped me off at Station 11. I was bussed directly to the MGM along with more fire fighters reporting in. Upon arrival at the scene I reported to C-3 (Chief Robert Atkinson) for assignment. He said he already had crews evacuating up to the 18th floor. I was to pick a crew and start evacuating from the 19th floor up to the top (26th floor).

The scene was one of unrivaled devastation and mayhem. The ground floor casino level was gutted by fire and was still burning. Thick black smoke was pouring upward through the structure. A steady stream of victims poured out of the building while firefighters poured in. Many, many people were still trapped on the upper floors, hanging out windows and standing on balconies screaming for help.

A few desperate people jumped to their deaths. Our ladder trucks could only reached the 9th floor and all elevators and electricity were out. Approximately 30 Engines with their crews fought the fire at the street level.

My job was to save people on the upper floors. Since we were off duty personnel, we had no real equipment. No air masks, no flashlights, and no radios. We entered the building with nothing but our personal fire gear (clothing) for protection and whatever else we could scrounge.

I picked a crew from the off duty personnel and we entered the building through the east end smokeless stairwell. It was eerie, black, and smoky. A steady stream of people were coming down, crying, screaming, and choking. We directed them and encouraged them while we continued to make our way to the 19th floor. At about the 10th floor, we encountered our first fatality. After a quick check, it was clear there was no helping him, so we continued on.

On the 14th floor I found an airpack without an air bottle. I carried it up with me hoping I would find a bottle of air higher up. I was lucky. At the 16th floor I found a full bottle. I put it together and found the pack even had a flashlight attached to it.

Finally on the 19th floor my crew began evacuation of each individual room. This was a monumental job when you consider that each floor has approximately 120 rooms and there are 26 floors. Some of the rooms of course were empty, the people had already fled, but many were still occupied by the terrified guests.

By now, the smoke was so dense in the stairwell and it was so far to ground level that we directed the people upward to the roof. Many helicopter crews, some military and some civilian had already started evacuation of people from the roof of the 26 story colossus.

On the 20th floor we started finding more bodies. The death toll grew as we continued upward. On the 23rd floor, my crew found 8 bodies piled in the hallway outside the elevator entrance. They died waiting in panic for an elevator that never arrived. The power was out.

We had no keys for all of the locked rooms, so we had to force and breakdown most of the doors to gain entry and check out the rooms. We cleared the 21st floor, but the door to room 2157 wouldn't budge, so we moved on to the 22nd floor. On the 22nd we started clearing rooms and from one of the balconies, we could see a woman laying out on the balcony from room 2157 below us. We returned to the 21st floor, battered down the door and found a terribly frightened woman, about 45 years old, with a broken leg explaining why she didn't come to the door while we were banging on it.

We splinted her lower leg using a bed slat and pillow and tied it with sheet strips. We tore off one of the bathrooms swinging doors to use as a backboard so we could carry her 5 stories up the stairwell to the roof where we deposited her to await evac.

We went back down to continue clearing rooms and realized we had a growing problem. A crew would finish clearing a floor and along comes another crew not knowing the floor had already been checked, repeating the effort. We devised a simple plan to insure that all rooms would be checked without duplication. We gathered together bars of soap from the bathrooms to use as marking pencils. I told the guys to be sure and mark the door of each room with an O.K. if they found it clear. After this we started making real headway and didn't have to search each room again and again.

Eventually, the evacuation effort was broken up into more specific areas for the crews. By noon we had completed clearing the entire south end tower down to the 6th floor.we had no idea how the actual fire fight was going and all we could do was hope the crews below were getting the fire under control. Along the way somewhere we were joined by two young men, MGM Employees, who worked as lifeguards in the Hotels pool area. They were a great help as they knew the layout of the Hotel making the job much, much easier. Their names were Jon Carpenter and John Luke. They continued to stick with me all day and into the evening.

1:00 p.m. - We made it back down to street level. The Salvation Army (God bless them!) had set up an aid station canteen for the firemen and other workers.

My head was pounding and felt like it would split. It must have been from the Carbon Monoxide. My body was blackened with smoke, eyes were red and running, and black ooze was dripping from my nose.

We took a short break, got a sandwich and a drink then got right back to it. I was now working on the Casino level and could see the devastation. The entire enormous main Casino, that only nine hours before had been filled with vacationers and tourists was completely gutted. The Hotels front entrance and canopy were gone. Burned out.

We continued to search for victims. We found many more bodies in the elevators, people who were trapped when the power went out. Three of the twenty elevators were found at ground level with dead in them. Other elevators were stuck throughout the high rise scattered on various floors. Many elevators told the story of grisly deaths for their riders. Husbands and wives were found still holding each others hands.

At about 3:00 p.m. we began assisting the coroner tag the bodies and take them to the roof area for helicopter removal. I was so tired, I knew I didn't want to climb the 26 stories again, so I caught a ride up to the roof on an Air Force Military Helicopter.

We were no longer rescuing, but recovering. I assisted in the removal of approximately 40 bodies, that had been discovered between the 16th and 26th floors. One rather large woman must have weighed around 200 pounds. We had to carry her up ten stories of the interior stairway from the 16th floor to the roof. Everyone was exhausted, but there were many more bodies that had to be moved.

5:00 p.m. - Darkness fell and it was extremely dark inside the hotels upper floors. I had dug up a good hand lantern and we kept on working by that light. We found ourselves working against an unfortunate deadline. For some reason by 6:30 p.m. the military helicopters could no longer assist us and would have to return to their bases. By almost exactly 6:30 p.m. we were able to remove the last of the bodies that we had found and could move. We were able to talk the pilot into making one more run, with us. We were able to load us and most of the fire fighting gear we had aboard that last flight and we considered ourselves lucky enough to scramble aboard for the last trip to the ground.

It was scary aboard that loaded helicopter in the darkness as it banked in the sky and headed to the ground. I couldn't help but to reflect on the fact that if that one engine failed or sputtered we would drop to the ground like a rock. The rest of the evening was spent doing mop up, removing hose, and recovering equipment.

During my day of searching, besides bodies, we also found drugs and money. This was turned in to the authorities. In the burned out Casino I found a stack of money, coins, chips, tokens that was literally 4 feet deep by 4 feet wide by 8 feet long. Armies of Hotel Security were removing the cash strong boxes from the Casino main cage area. Money was everywhere, just as it had been left when the wall of flame swept through the Casino.

I salvaged two burned tokens as a symbol of all that had happened there that day and as a reminder to myself that sometimes the forces of nature are more than we can handle. So far the death toll is 84. That number may grow, if victims at the local hospitals pass. The dollar loss is certainly in the multi-millions of dollars. I am sure it will be regarded as the single largest catastrophe in a single building in modern times, but the toll in lives and suffering could never have a value placed on it.

I can't help thinking of the terror and suffering of the people trapped in the elevators, knowing that they were sitting on the ground floor so close to escape.

9:30 p.m. - At the end of the long day, when I was released from the fire scene, I was dropped off at my home by another fireman. All my children and my wife ran out to great me. I was tired and dirty, but I sure felt blessed. It was good to be alive.

This was written by Chief RB Taylor the Day after the Fire.

****

Captain Jim Perkins, Station 21, C Platoon

Clark County Fire Department, Las Vegas, Nevada

Well Pauly, where do I begin. Interesting stories. You know, if you could have caught me maybe ten years ago I would still have some memory left, but I'll do my best.

The MGM Grand fire. I was off duty the day the MGM Hotel fire came down. I happened to be stationed at station 11, across the street, so all my gear was close by.

Firefighters were arriving in droves. We got there in the street, and were faced by mayhem even outside the Hotel. Flamingo Road, in front of the MGM, was completely blocked up with fire vehicles and cars that had just stopped in the middle of the road. Pedestrians, and firemen were everywhere. There was someone out in the street with a bullhorn trying to maintain some kind of order, without much luck.

There was no, real, effective communications, and no structural organization to our fire fighting slash rescue effort. At that time we didn't have the Incident Command System so it was more or less management by chaos, especially from the firefighters perspective.

I got on scene about the same time as a bunch of other guys. I was the head of a team we had at that time called the High Angle Rescue Team (HART) and so my assignment was to evacuate and assist in evacuation of the upper floors of the high rise. We were given an assignment but no radio, and no med bags. We had basically just a coil of rope and a real small first aid kit. Just basic, bandage type first aid.

The stairwells were clogged with people retreating from heavy smoke. There were only two of us from the HART Team at first. Myself and John Jersey. We were picked up in a military helicopter in the parking lot and flown above the structure where we were then lowered down on a winch type thing to a sixteenth floor balcony.

We entered the building from the balcony and started down the hallway. The hallways were lined with pictures of movie stars, I remember going down those hallways and thinking those pictures seemed odd and out of place now. It was very dark and there was thick soot on everything. We came up to the elevator lobby and found a pile of people. As I remember it, there was eight to ten victims there, some with their arms around each other. They were all right there in front of the elevator doors. They were all very dead. We did a brief check for signs of life. Nothing. We were basically in a kind of shock while trying to triage the situation.

More firefighters had joined us and we would search from room to room,. There was probably about six of us by this time. What we would do was go from room to room marking the doors of the rooms we had searched with a bar of soap. We would get anybody that was ambulatory out of the room and gather them into one room that had decent air still in it. We left one person in charge while the rest of us kept herding all the people up there along.

Once we had about 20 people gathered together, we would take the them up to the roof in a group, carrying the ones that couldn't walk by themselves, and trust me, a lot of them had to be carried. We would take them up the stairs to the roof. We only had one center stairwell that was kind of clear of smoke so that's where we went. From the roof the victims would be evacuated by helicopter down to the ground. This went on over and over, floor by floor.

The disaster was fickle. I remember one room where we had an elderly couple, were laying in the bathroom. They had used wet rags to combat the smoke. They were both dead. In the very next room there were four couples in their pajamas, and they were sitting around drinking tequila and playing cards at the coffee table.

Fire hadn't made it to any of the upper floors. There was only smoke Deadly, deadly smoke. When you look back on it, you can see that the building acted like one big chimney. People heard the fire alarms and went for the stairwells or the elevators. Unfortunately, that's where the heavy toxic smoke was coming up from, and right where those people died.

The smoke and soot was very thick and very heavy throughout the whole building, but you could always find a somewhat clear room, as long as that outside window was intact. Smoke was coming up the outside of the building as well as working its way up on the inside. As long as the windows and doors hadn't been breached in the room, the room was pretty safe. So you'd find one room like I said, where everyone was partying, and having fun, and in the next room, you'd have a couple of dead bodies. It went that way all through the whole operation.

At one point, Bob Barret was screaming out for help. He had been with a victim that had just stopped breathing. He was yelling out for airway kits and Defibrillators and everything else. Of course, we didn't have any of that stuff with us, and had no access to it. We couldn't really render any kind of medical aid to anybody. If they were ambulatory we could get them out of the building. If they weren't ambulatory, we could carry them. If they were in a situation where we normally could have helped them, there wasn't to much we could do for them here. It was a very tense, emotionally charged situation.

The people we came across were generally not panicky. They walked around in kind of a state of shock. We would walk them down the hallways which were littered with bodies, especially near the elevators, to a clear room, and then up and out.

We went floor by floor, from the sixteenth floor on up. We worked all through the day. Around 4:00 in the afternoon, I finally made it up to the roof with a load of patients and I looked down to the parking lot. There were several helicopters down there with their rotors turning, you could see smoke all over and big crowds of people. There were injured down on the ground and mayhem everywhere. I couldn't help but think this was Vietnam all over again. With all the military helicopters and medivacs going on, it really did look like a war zone.

I met up with Billy Porter up on the roof. We decided that we had had enough. We had already cleared the floors from the sixteenth on up to the roof, so we jumped onto one of the helicopters and got a ride down to the ground. We walked across the street to Station 11's parking lot, got in Billies car and headed out to get a break and something to eat.

There was very little accountability at this scene. Firefighters came and went at will. It was kind of, by necessity, a cowboy operation. For the firefighting efforts out front and operations on the ground, it may have been a little bit different, but certainly the activities that went on in the towers were strictly cowboy operations. No contact with the outside. If anything had happened to us, we couldn't even call for help. It was all disorienting, and very, very confusing.

We managed to move hundreds of people out of that building, either on to the roof, or down to the ground safely. The eighty four people that we didn't get out, the ones I personally saw, effected my life more than any other one thing.

I am a strong supporter of Critical Incident Stress Debriefings, ever since that aweful day. I have seen the damage that fire did both to myself and my firefighting brothers. It was a very difficult situation. Something I will always remember. Some of it I remember like it was yesterday, and other things I hope I never remember.

Bill Trelease and I were talking about this the other day. We remembered that on the eighteenth floor, somebody had been desperately pushing the button for the elevator. There were several dead people there right in front of the elevator doors. You could actually see where their hand had gone up to push the button. Their hands had left marks up and down the wall. The soot was so thick, you could actually see the finger marks on the wall.

After the call, I was so sore from smashing in doors. I tried a kick method, shoulder method, run into it with your back method, picking up big ashtrays that were in the hallway and bashing the door method, and just about every other method you could imagine. The doors were big heavy doors, and it really took a lot of effort to force them open. For about a week, I was blowing black snot out from my nose, from the soot. My hair at that time was quite blonde. When I came out, my hair was completely black.

If you ever make a movie from your book, and Costner's in it, and you need me to double, let me know. I'll do it for nothing buddy.

****

Captain Paul Young, Station 18, C Platoon
   Clark County Fire Department, Las Vegas, Nevada

The day of the MGM Fire I was working as a Paramedic for the local ambulance company. I was just getting off the morning of the fire after a 24 hour shift when the phone rang. It was dispatch. They said that they had a fire going at the MGM Grand and that they wanted us to move in closer to the strip area.

Initially we thought "Oh yea. No big deal. They always have fires. Little grease fires in kitchens and things." They usually never amount to anything. That morning, as we got into the rig, we saw this hugh column of smoke coming up from the south and we knew. "Oh boy! This is the real deal this time!"

We started heading towards the MGM, got off the freeway at Flamingo and of course by then there was a mass of fire apparatus everywhere you looked. There were hose lines covering the ground, the total definition of spaghetti. The Strip by now was closed off to traffic. I remember the column of smoke going up in the air. People were running around like their heads were cut off. It was total chaos. The ICS System really didn't exist back then, and there wasn't really a true kind of direction or leadership in place. From what I could see people were just running everywhere trying to figure out how to go about commanding this massive fire.

I remember one of my first assignments was to work a cardiac arrest patient in the middle of Flamingo and Las Vegas Boulevard. We were doing CPR on this guy even though we had limited medical help on scene. We really didn't have enough medical help to commit an entire unit to this one cardiac arrest patient. I just thought what a joke. It may sound heartless, but we had thousands of people exiting the hotel, pouring out all covered in soot and in all various forms of dress, suffering from every type of injury, from the minor to major, but they wanted us to focus this one patient.

Someone finally realized we couldn't save everyone and said "Hey, this guy is dead…we gotta move on to the living". So we covered this guy up with a sheet and left him laying there in the middle of Flamingo and Las Vegas Boulevard.

In an odd moment, I remember a Doctor on scene who came running up to me and asked me if I would radio my dispatcher and have them call his answering service because his beeper went off and he couldn't make out the message. He actually wanted our dispatcher, at the height of the fire to find out what his beeper message was! Needless to say, I blew him off, and he vanished into the crowd, never to be seen again.

I clearly remember all the people pouring out of the building like ants looking for a crumb, They were looking for direction, looking for a place to go. No one seemed to have any answers for them. We transported so many people, load after load, after load. Most of them suffering from smoke inhalation, sprains, knee twist and such. It was complete insanity

Once a plan of attack took form, Clark County School buses began shuttleing the walking wounded and the non-injured over to one of the halls at the Convention Center. They were taking them there as a kind of triage, or holding pen until they were able to relocate these people.

This became the place the people could meet and gather with their loved ones, seek minor medical attention and such. We responded to the Convention Center for a medical call. This nurse came running up to the rig in a total panic, with hair frayed, hyperventilating and just totally at wits end. She comes over to my side of the rig and says "We're over there in that corner." pointing in a vague direction over a sea of people. "I want you to come over and bring all the Morphine you've got." She turned around and then ran back into the crowd. We never saw her again!

The high point of the insanity for us came on a call nowhere near the MGM. We were at the hospital after having taken a load of patients, when we got called to respond to a home way out near the intersection of Hollywood and Lake Mead area, Back in those days this was a pretty remote area. The call was to this big house all by itself up on Sunrise Mountain.

The patient was an MGM Stockholder. We found out later that he was a pretty important businessman in town and he had a lot of MGM Grand stock. When he saw the fire, I guess for whatever reason...Afraid of losing stock money or what, I don't know...he shot himself in the head. Shot himself right there at the height of the MGM fire. Go figure.

CHAPTER 9

"This is when I started crying. I had just realized that I was almost able to save these kids dad so that they wouldn't be orphans."

EJECTED

Fire Fighter BJ Velez - Branchville Volunteer Fire Company, Station 11

Prince George's County Fire Department, Maryland

This isn't the worst call I have ever been on but it is the one that sticks out in my head the most.

My name is BJ Velez. I am currently a fire fighter / E.M.T. for the Branchville Vol. Fire Company and Rescue Squad. This is in Prince George's County, MD and is Station #11 of the Prince George's County Fire Department.

I was originally a volunteer in New York State where the fire service and Rescue services were seperate, so when I moved to Maryland where the services are combined, I was forced to take EMT training. I started to put in time on the Ambulance. After completing my E.M.T. class and was soon turned over to ride as an aid man for my department (A primary care provider on the ambulance). I had been on my share of car wrecks and medical emergencies, but now I was the main person responsible. Peoples lives were actually in my hands

About one week after being turned over, we received a call for an overturned car on I-95 South right before the Capital Beltway (I-495). My driver and I were first out of the station with the engine following after.

While enroute Communications notified us that a Prince George Police Officer was on the scene and was reporting that five people had been ejected. We arrived on the scene and could not believe what we saw. There were three kids screaming and crying and all of the victims had been ejected some 50 to 100 feet away from their vehicle. Down the way, I could see the Police Officer preforming CPR on what I later found out to be the children's mother.

Despite my limited experience I knew that since I was the first emergency medical person on the scene I would need to establish a priority as to who we would treat first and who could wait for other medical personnel. As tough as it made things, Hearing the kids screaming was actually a good sign. Quiet kids in traumatic accidents is all bad, and is often an indicator of very serious injuries.

I had asked the Officer how long he had been working on the mother and he replied that he had been going for about 15 minutes with no response, and that her bones all felt crushed. I found the father about 50 feet away. He had a weak pulse which actually stopped while I was checking him. I then made him my priority.

I started to preform CPR on the dad as the Engine arrived. My driver had radioed back to Communications with advising them of the situation and calling for additional help. After 2 to 3 minutes of CPR, I was able to get back a weak pulse on the Dad. Both I and the other Emergency Medical Personnel were amazed and excited about it!

As we loaded the Father into the back of the Medic Unit, we lost his pulse again. The Paramedics took over his care, but eventually pronounced him. I had moved on to help with the kids. All three were all stable, but badly injured. A helicopter had been called to air lift the kids to Children's Hospital in DC. As they were bringing the last kid to the chopper, a little girl, a Maryland State Trooper gave the frightened child a Teddy Bear. As the flight crew loaded her into the chopper, the little girl said thank you and waved goodbye.

This is when I started crying. It hit me that I was almost able to save these kids dad so that they wouldn't be orphans. News cameras were flooding to the scene, so I just slinked back to my Ambulance.

Turns out that the family was from New York and were on there way to a family reunion in Ohio. An eye witness said that he saw the families truck swerving for several miles before the accident. I guess the driver had fallen asleep.

I still think to myself about what happened to those little kids and how they are dealing without their parents. I can still see the little girls with her Teddy Bear. It makes me feel fortunate that I still have my parents. I also know that at anytime I could lose them. Maybe even in the same way these kids lost there parents.

SERGEANT CARTER
Fire Fighter Bobby Hunter

Sergeant John M. Carter was a career fire fighter with the D.C. Fire Department and a volunteer with the Kensington Volunteer Fire Department. I went to fire courses and became good friends with Johns nephew, so John's death hit me pretty hard.

On October 24th, 1997 at 06:20, a call came in to D.C's dispatch reporting smoke in the area of 400 Kennedy St NW. A second call indicated heavy smoke coming from a building and the response was upgraded to a full building fire response.

The first arriving units began an aggressive attack on the fire, but the fire got a good foothold before crews arrived. The raging fire was making the building very dangerous as flames were eating holes in the floors. Due to the condition of the building, the intense heat, and the heavy fire condition, crews were forced to pull out and go defensive. Engine 14's crew worked their way out only to notice that one of their men, Sergeant Carter wasn't with them.

Frantic, they reentered the building to find Carter - with no luck. The fire fight went on. Heavy master streams were used to pour massive amounts of water on the blaze while crews continued to try and search for Sergeant Carter, again with no luck. Over 90 minutes after going missing, Carter was found by a crew in the basement. They found him pinned under some debris.

As the Body of Sergeant John Carter was removed from the building, all operations stopped and every fire fighters eyes and hearts turned to their fallen brother.

A few days later, Sergeant Carter was laid to rest. Thousands of uniformed personnel from around the world attended. As the funeral procession moved down the long road to Carters final resting spot, fire and rescue personnel stood stock still at attention besides their units. Engine 14 carried Carters body.

The casket was laid in its final spot and the heart of every firefighter was filled with sadness.

Almost a year later, a report was released detailing the death of Sergeant Carter. The report stated that Sergeant Carter had fallen through one of the many holes in the floor and that he was alive and alert after his fall. Sergeant Carter had attempted a call for help saying "Engine 14's in the basement" This transmission wasn't heard by the communications center.

Sergeant Carter died by drowning. After falling through the floor, the fire fighting effort continued to pour thousands of gallons per minute into the building. The water used to battle the fire flooded the basement, taking the life of an American Hero.

SPECIAL DELIVERY
Engineer / Paramedic Warren Whitney - Station 12, C Platoon
Clark County Fire Department, Las Vegas, Nevada

It was the fourth of July. The Las Vegas valley was partying hard. It had been a long shift so far, but this call would be the oddest of the night.

We were dispatched to a report of a suicide attempt. In a place like Vegas, not the most unusual call. We pulled up to the address and were met by a neighbor. she said that she had found the gentleman in the garage with the engine of his car running. We found a man in his fifties laying on the floor of the garage next to his still running car.

The gentleman as it turned out would be fine. He seemed to be nothing more than drunk. On the hood of the car we spotted a Fed-Ex envelope. Thinking it might contain a suicide note or something, we took a look inside. We soon wished we hadn't done that. Inside the envelope was the largest pile of shit you have ever seen!

The story started to unfold. This had not been a suicide attempt at all. The gentleman had been out partying very, very, very hard, and was on his way home. He was apparently hit by a sudden uncontrollable urge to crap and decided it was easier to fill the envelope rather then stop and find a bathroom. he pulled into his driveway in a drunken blur, running over some decorative bushes on the way in. He took his shit filled envelope and stumbled out of the car (forgetting to turn off the engine) and then quickly passed out on the garage floor.

PRAY FOR MY BABY
Fire Fighter Jason Neuman

Probably the saddest call I ever responded to was a traffic accident (Rollover) with two patients ejected. An 18 month old girl and her mother. The Father walked away with only minor injuries. As we arrived on the scene, a quick triage was conducted. We approached our first patient, the child, who was pulseless and apnic. She had an obvious head injury with blood coming from both ears and the nose. I think you get the picture.

We issued the little girl a black tag indicating the she was dead. A few greens Which meant the patient could wait for care were distributed and Mom received a red tag to indicate that she was a priority patient due to her serious injuries. We assisted the paramedics with the Mother while the other Engine Company on scene assisted the victims in another vehicle.

We told the Father that his wife was being transported to the hospital. He didn't respond. He continued to stare in the direction where his daughter still lay. He got up then walked over to his daughters lifeless body, kneeled down and said, "I need to pray for my baby". I didn't know how to respond or what to do. They don't teach you this in the academy. I just put my hand on his shoulder.

When we returned to the Station, a Critical Incident Stress Debriefing Counselor was at the Station to discuss the incident with the personnel who responded. I guess calls like this always hit home no matter how tough or how strong you are. I know I speak for every emergency responder. I hope I never respond to another incident involving a child for the rest of my career.

Well Paul, I'm going to take a break. I have a few amusing stories. In the mean time, best of luck to you.

DOWN ON THE FARM
Fire Fighter Shaun Bean
Liberal Fire Department, Liberal, Missouri

My name is Shaun Bean I work full time for the Barton County Ambulance District in Lamar Missouri. I also work part time for the Vernon County Ambulance District in Nevada Missouri. My wife Sandy works part time for both districts as a paramedic. I also am a volunteer fire fighter for the Liberal Fire Department which is located in Liberal. We live in a quite rural area. My oldest child is also a trained first responder. I guess you might say she is a chip off the old block.

I was off duty and responded to a call at a friends farm for an injured child. I was the first EMS worker on scene. The child's head had been run over by the rear tire of a four wheel drive combine.

A shear feeling of total helplessness comes to you with a call like this. Knowing that there was nothing I could do that would save this child. CPR had already been started so we had to go through the whole process even though in our hearts we knew there was no hope. A doctor arrived on the scene in a relatively short amount of time and called the code right there.

I still have trouble thinking about this call. Calls with kids are always tough but this was worse as it was a farm accident and I'm a farmer too. I probably will never forget holding the crushed head of that small child, trying to keep his airway open. The tragedy greatly affected my wife as she taught the child in a program at school. I know I will certainly never forget it.

FATHER
Fire Fighter Shaun Bean
Liberal Fire Department, Liberal, Missouri

I was on duty the morning that my own father had a massive heart attack and died.

You know when you take a job like ours, that you may end up taking care of a friend or family member, but you protect yourself by thinking "it will never happen to me". I guess when I reflect on this day, what gets to me the most is that I took this job to help people and to try and save lives, yet on one of the most important calls of my life, there was nothing to be done. There was nothing I could do to save my fathers life.

There were two Medics on scene along with my wife and I. We were only five minutes away from the hospital, but here was just nothing that could be done. Sometimes life just ends.

As hard as it was, my wife and I were able to focus and do our jobs. We gave it our all. We were able to hold our emotions in until the very moment that Dad was declared dead at the hospital. The next morning, we had to go home and tell my kids that their Grandfather was gone.

Well I guess that is about it. I don't know if you can use this or not. Good luck on your book even if you don't use this. If you don't mind let me know how your book goes. Thanks for listening to me.

ANTS

Captain Paul Youdelis - Station 12, C Platoon
Clark County Fire Department, Las Vegas, Nevada

We responded on a 419 (Dead Body) call. apparently, the gentleman had been dead for quite sometime. These calls are always great fun.

We arrived and were met by a friend who had found him. He was laying on the kitchen floor, wearing nothing but a T shirt and underpants. There was spilt coffee grounds on the counter and the floor. It seemed like he had gotten out of bed one morning and dropped dead while making his morning coffee.

Judging by the newspapers in the driveway, he had been there for about 5 days. We had entered the house through a garage door. We didn't need to check for a pulse or respirations, as one look at him confirmed that he was in fact dead. I was about to head back out to wait for the police and the coroner when I noticed a black line on the floor. I turned and followed the line back into the house where the line split in two. One running to the head of the victim and the other to his butt. I thought to myself..."What the hell is this." I looked closer and was disgusted to find that it wasn't a line, but an army of ants! half going in his mouth, half going in his ass.

BLOWN AWAY
Fire Fighter Chris Ridgell
Landis Fire Department, North Carolina

I don't know if you can use it, but I went on a call that absolutely horrified me. I've only been in the fire service for a few years but I've had several fire fighters and chief officers tell me that they have never seen anything like this in their career.

I am on a volunteer fire department here in North Carolina. One morning at about 4:00 a.m. or so, we were dispatched to give mutual aid for a gas leak. A tree had fallen across the road during a storm and blocked access to the home where the problem was. The incident commander on-scene advised us to come in from the opposite side of the street for access.

About 2 blocks away from the house, we could already smell the natural gas heavy in the air. The tree that had fallen had ruptured the gas line that fed the house. Once we arrived on scene, the incident commander called on the radio and told us he needed us to don our SCBA and investigate the gas leak since crews on his side couldn't get close enough due to the tree and some downed power lines.

On our engine, we had an engineer, assistant chief, lieutenant, and myself (then a "probie"). Being the bottom two on the "totem pole", the lieutenant and I donned our SCBA and proceeded up to the house. We had gotten about ten to twelve feet from the house when all of a sudden, something ignited the leaking gas.

The explosive fireball flashed through the house and the pressure blew one side of the house away. The force of the explosion was so powerful, it lifted the entire roof off of the house and sent it into the air. The right side of the house (the side we were approaching) disintegrated and scattered debris all around us. Of course, we just knew we were dead. In the end, no one was hurt and we finally got the gas leak under control.

Happy to be alive, I got back to my house, called my wife at her job and told her I was OK and that I loved her very very much.

THE HUG
Fire Fighter Bobby Hunter

It was a warm summer afternoon and a light rain had just finished falling. The sounds of summer were interrupted by the beeps of my fire radio... "Personnel Injury Accident" (Car Accident). The call was just a block away so I decided to go.

I arrived on the scene to find a two car accident One of the cars landed in someones front yard and the other was mangled into a Guard rail. I approached the car in the yard and found an older woman with a major laceration to the head above her eyes. She was understandably frightened and quite disoriented.

I needed to know the condition of the people in the other car before I could decide who to treat first, so I went over to the other car and was horrified to find a Mother and her children in the torn up car. Through the shattered windshield I could see a 3 year old girl laying on the front passenger floor. Her 5 year old sister was crying in the front passengers seat with a large bump on her head. She seemed to have almost no movement in her legs and was in extreme pain. In the drivers seat was the hysterical mother. She dazed but was still trying to pull her self to her children.

I was the only Emergency worker on the scene and it was impossible for me to hold C Spine on all of the patients. With the Fire Department coming from over 3 miles up the road I started t recruit help. I asked a bystander to grab a towel and hold it over the cut on the older ladies head while I began to hold C Spine on the restless 5 year old.

The mothers condition had begun to deteriorate. she started to float in and out of conciseness. I continued to hold traction on the 5 year old while trying to talk to the mother to keep her conscious. I did my very best to keep an eye on the 3 year old between my feet to see if she was still breathing and conscious.

Time seemed to stand still until the Chief arrived. I gave him the rundown on what we had - four patients, all currently trapped in their vehicles at the time. Other firefighters arrived and the extrication process began. I fought to hold back tears of frustration as the sounds of the Hurst Tool scared the children even more then they already were.

Two helicopters were brought in. I stayed with the 5 year old the entire time until she was loaded in the chopper. I felt like if I left her, she would just have no one. I learned a lot about the pretty little 5 year old that day. Oddly enough, she was friends with my little cousin. After over 45 minutes, all four patients were on their way to the hospital.

A couple of days later we received some follow up information about the accident. everyone involved had been released from the hospital and were at home healing. The 5 year old regained movement in her legs later that night.

Weeks later I went to pick up my cousin from school and as I walked into the classroom I got the surprise of a lifetime! The little girl who stole my heart that day, walked up to me and gave me a hug!! I couldn't believe that after everything she had been through she remembered me. Minutes later her mother came in and she told her mom who I was; She thanked me for being there for her daughter when she was by herself, and for being so caring.

This was the perfect ending to something that could of had a much different turnout. To this day, this is the most memorable call for me and one that I'll never forget.

A NIGHT OF PRAYING
Fire Fighter Bobby Hunter

Every fire fighters worst nightmare is that they will get hurt or even die on a call.

This particular night, that fear came true. It was 10 o'clock on December 8, 1995. The night before our Department's Christmas party. The nightly news was just coming on. There had been a big warehouse fire in Washington D.C earlier that evening. The news reporters said that the fire had been burning for over 4 hours and that it was still not under control. He also spoke the words that echoed through many fire stations and hearts, "There were some injury's in the blaze. One civilian and two Firefighters have been injured." Their condition was still unknown.

It was around 4:15 p.m. when a civilian knocked on the door of D.C Engine 12's door to report the fire in the warehouse at the corner of 5th and V streets NE. Only a half block from Engine 12's quarters. At 4:16 the D.C Fire Dispatch Center sent out the Box Alarm..."5th and V streets NE, Building fire , Engines 4, 6, 17, 26, Trucks 4, 15, Battalion 1 and Rescue Squad 2."

Engine 12 was out on a Medical Call at the time so they weren't dispatched. The warehouse was a two story building and was filled with tire's from floor to Ceiling on both floor's.

Battalion 1 requested a working fire dispatch which added Engine 2, Battalion 6, Metro Support (Air Unit), Car 43(FM), Medic 17 and Ambulance 25. At 4:22 pm, heavy fire was showing from the roof so Battalion 1 now requested a second alarm which brought Engines 11 , 14, 18, 24, Chief Seavey's company Engine 16, Truck 3, Truck 9, Battalion 4, the Mobile Command Unit and the Canteen Unit.

The massive fire continued to demand more units so at 4:33 a request for the Foam Unit Task Force, Foam 1 and 2 responded.

Eventually Engines 9, 12, 21, Trucks 6 and 7 and the Naval District of Washington Foam 1 and 2 responded making it a third alarm.

Engine 16 under the Command of Chief James Seavey took position in a school bus parking lot along with Truck 6. As Truck 6 moved into position, the supply line laying across the entrance way got entangled in the dual rear wheel's of the truck. The hose went airborne and struck Chief Seavey in the back and tossing him in the air. He said, "it felt like I was hit by a Mack Truck. When I dawned on me that I couldn't move part of my body, I thought that I'd be viewing Fire trucks from a Wheelchair for the rest of my life."

An Ambulance took Chief Seavey to the Trauma Center at the Washington Hospital Center. I was at home with my mom and dad watching the fire on TV when the phone rang, it was my Grandmother calling. She had heard from someone at the firehouse that Seavey was in the Hospital. My dad called the firehouse to find out all the detail's. I waited nervously as he Talked on the phone. Chief Seavey had always been like a father to me even before I joined the Fire Department.

That night we all prayed that he would get better and be back soon. Chief Seavey was Paralyzed from the neck down for 16 hours. He spent over 25 hours in the Trauma Center before being taken to a regular Hospital.

Seavey stayed in that hospital until December 12th before finally being released. He returned to Light Duty on January 17, 1996, where he stayed for over a year. During that time, he was utilized as an instructor at the Fire Academy.

There were two more injury's that night, one was another Firefighter who suffered from Smoke Inhalation (he was released from the Hospital later that night) and the other was a Security Guard who had also been hit by the same hose as Seavy. He was treated and released at the scene.

The fire burned for 36 hours and an Engine Company stayed for an additional 24 hours as a fire watch.

The Christmas Party that year was dedicated to Chief Seavey, We all missed him at the party the following night. You can't imagine how glad we were to see him come back to work both as a D.C Firefighter and as the Chief at Cabin John Fire Department.

TAKING A DIP

Captain Jim Perkins - Station 23, C Platoon
Clark County Fire Department, Las Vegas, Nevada

I had been on for about 6 months and was running out of Station 18. It was around October or November of 1974. We were called out on a multiple alarm fire on Susan and Ida. I was riding rescue 18 and my partner at the time was John Wood. The buildings near Susan and Ida were commonly a square layout. These were 2 story buildings with a center courtyard that had a swimming pool taking up most of it. The entrances to the courtyard were a kind of tunnel that went from the parking area, under the second story and into the first floor area and courtyard/pool area.

We could see the flames and smoke when we pulled out of the station. Fire had already vented out the roof by the time we got there. The fire was pretty much confined to one apartment at the east end. Engine 11 arrived first, pulled lines and got a real quick knock down on the fire. As I said, I was on a rescue and the rescue carried all of the salvage gear at that time so my partner and I went in and started running lights around the second floor.

We were up there doing our thing, when someone noticed that there was still smoke issuing from the roof, so they set up the stick and started pouring water in the hole where the fire had vented.

In just a matter of seconds, the Captain from Engine 11, Don Stowe, started to scream for everyone to get out. We ran out of the room where we had been stringing lights and we could see that flames were shooting down out of the rafters, had consumed the roof of the breezeway, and were in fact pushing out of the structure anywhere they could all the way around the building. The water from the tower had pushed unseen fire all through the attic and voids. It was spreading so fast that all we could do was get crews out of the building.

I was up on the balcony with Captain Stowe and John Wood. John bailed out of the building while Captain Stowe and I took up a line and started to put some water on the fire to provide some cover for the fleeing crews. What we didn't realize was that the fire was rolling over the breezeway entrance a little bit more than we thought it was. Without warning the whole entrance area just collapsed and cut our line off.

Everything was ripping pretty good by now, with flames shooting up to about 50 or 75 feet or so around us. We were pretty much up shit creek. We ran over to the only place of refuge, the pool and jumped in. We didn't wear airpacks at that time so we didn't have those to worry about. We just hopped in the pool! There we were just sitting in the water with just the tops of our helmets, eyes, and noses peeking out over the water line.

The heat was very intense. We just sat in the pool watching the air conditioners blow, little fireballs were blowing into the courtyard, burning lumber was crashing down around us, and we just sat in the pool as the whole thing burned to the ground around us. I guess we cooled our heels in the pool for about an hour. Don just kept making jokes the whole time.

When crews were finally able to get in, I knew they expected to find bodies, after all we had been missing for a very long time. Our helmets were melted on our heads and we had to have them cut from our hair. Other than that, we came out just fine. Soggy, but fine.

EVEN MORE QUICKIES

Fire Fighter Brian Fullerton

Westbrook Fire Fighters, Windham, Maine

Here are a few stories from my 35 years of service. Like I told you on the phone, I'll have 36 years in July 6th. I'm going to the end of the year then retire. I wish you great luck with your book. Please take care and be safe.

1968 - Early one morning we responded to a house fire on Harrisburg Avenue. A small ranch house was fully involved, and fire was coming out of every window. When the fire was under control, most of the inside had been gutted. What we found in the living room was unreal! Sitting in what had been a recliner was a skeleton of the elderly man who had lived there. It was discovered by the State Fire Marshall that the old man probably feel asleep while smoking. I will never forget that one!

****

1999 - Captain Chapman was coming back from Portland. He saw a man face down off of the sidewalk at the entrance to the Maine Turnpike. He thought the man had been hit by a car so he called for a Rescue. When he got up to the man, he could smell the booze. The man was rapped up in a sign that said "Will work for food!". He was transported to the Hospital and was back on the street two days later.

****

1972 - "Of creatures great and small..." The call was box 21 at Main and Rochester. The first arriving Engine reported a working fire at Petits

Animal Hospital. A gallant attempt was made by the fire fighters to save the cats, dogs, and birds that were locked in their pens. But all were lost. This was an arson fire. Someone broke down the rear door and splashed gasoline inside the building, then torched it. Who could do that to those defenseless animals?

****

My late friend Glen "Smoky" Hodgkins would show up every year for fire prevention week dressed in a Smoky the Bear suit. At Christmas time, he would be Santa Clause. We were visiting Prides Corner School during fire prevention week with Glen dressed as Smoky. Here he comes, walking down the isle when he blurts out..."Ho, ho, ho!" He immediately realized what he had said then exclaimed "Opps! Wrong guy!"

****

We responded to a house on Brackett Street on a night in 1980. A young man distraught over a love affair gone bad had decided to kill himself with a wire cloths hanger. He had the hanger around his neck with the end of it inside a cordless drill. When we got there the drill was still running but had bound up. He was still alive but had a permanent scar around his neck. He is still living and his friends call him "Necklace".

****

We went to a house on Bridge Street for a man who tried to hang himself in his garage. He put a noose over his head with the rope tied to a beam; and jumped off of a chair. When we got there he was standing on the floor on his tip toes. The rope was still tied to his neck. He had the rope too long. He said once he jumped he had changed his mind.

****

Arthur Crow called to report a Blackbird that was caught in High Power wires. The next day, the newspaper reported that "A Crow reported, A blackbird caught in the wires."

****

We responded to a street box one summer day. When coming around the corner we saw a 1 or 2 year old child hanging from the fire box handle. After taking the child down, we found out the baby sitter had pulled the box and hung the child there.

THE EXPLODING TOILET
Assistant Chief John Mizia
Peters Township Fire Company, McMurray, Pennsylvania

I am the Assistant Chief of the Peters Township Fire Company in McMurray Pennsylvania. I have held that office for 25 years and have been a fire fighter for 29 years. I recently read a copy of your request for different fire calls faced by fire fighters. I have responded to many serious and fatal alarms. I would like to respond to your category of funniest. We have all run on the funny call, I have responded to some comical alarms that include: tree house fires, snake fires, people handcuffed to refrigerators and my all time favorite was a toilet explosion.

At approximately three a.m. one morning the tones dropped for a toilet explosion in a residential neighborhood. At first I thought that I was dreaming. After the repeated announcement, I decided that it was for real.

To make a long story short. A woman who was half asleep got up around three in the morning to relieve herself. When she was finished, she reached back and pulled the flush handle. At that point hot water (almost steam) from a malfunctioning hot water heater which had overheated the entire water piping system (hot & cold) began to refill the tank. When the hot water hit the cold china tank, the tank cracked and burst apart. The hot water also cracked the base of the toilet and it too fell to pieces. At that point the boiling hot water was shooting everywhere.

Needless to say the woman awakened quickly and called the fire department. The fire department had the lady checked by the medics and shut off the water supply and the hot water heater. She was uninjured, but like us, had a great story to tell. This is a true story. Good luck with your book

CHAPTER 10

"He brought up the camera and there almost at my feet was a balled up, glowing image of a human being."

LUCKY DAY

Captain Paul Youdelis - Station 12, C Platoon
Clark County Fire Department, Las Vegas, Nevada

It was early, and we had just started our shift. Our Rescue unit rolled out to a nearby hotel for a medical call. Shortly after, we rolled in the Engine also to a medical call. There was a report of a man down on Las Vegas Boulevard. It would prove to be one young woman's good fortune that this call was out on the street and not to far from our station.

We arrived to find a young man passed out drunk on the sidewalk. For us, this was a pretty routine call, so I stayed in the engine while my firefighters went to talk to the young man. I noticed a fire call come across the MCT and the address seemed to be right near my station so I clicked the call on my computer screen to see what was happening. Another big break for a very lucky lady.

The notes flashed onto the screen.

"Fire in the building, Ste 231, Big complex

Smoke and flames throughout the bldg.

2 trapped, more thought to be in bldg

Multi callers"

I was taken aback by the notes, but more so by the address. This building was directly across the street from our station that we just left!

I yelled out to my guys to turn the patient over to the ambulance crew and added us to the dispatch. From the time we were added to the call to our arrival was still less than one minute but in that minute the situation managed to get much worse.

The dispatchers were on the phone with a young woman who was trapped on the second floor in an unknown, windowless room. Dispatch advised she was coughing and crying. The victim said smoke was getting into the room and that she could here the hallway outside collapsing. The desperate woman had just informed the dispatcher that she was having trouble breathing when the phone line went dead.

On arrival we had heavy smoke showing from the South end of the building and from a breezeway about halfway down the length of the structure. Heavy fire was issuing from the South end roof and stairwell. I called for a 2nd alarm and transferred command to the second arriving engine so we could go into a rescue operation.

My crew and I pulled a long crosslay and joined with the firefighters from the second in engine and began to fight our way up the burning stairs. Visibility was almost zero and the stairwell was so hot it was burning holes into the initial line. We fought our way up to the second floor and left a team on the line while the rest of of began a search for the trapped woman.

I had just forced about my third door and entered the dark, smoke filled room when I thought I heard a weak voice coming from deep in the room. I shouted out and was sure I heard a reply, so I started to work my way deep into the room. I was calling for one of my firefighters who was behind me with a thermal imager to catch up. He brought up the camera and there almost at my feet was a balled up, glowing image of a human being.

I grabbed her and quickly and reassured her (amazed that she was still conscious as heavily smoke charged as the room was!). She said she couldn't walk, so my firefighter and I each got up under her arms and whisked her out of the room, through the destroyed hallway, down the gutted, hot stairs and out of the building to the rescue unit that was waiting for us.

The young woman survived with relatively minor injuries and smoke inhalation. Despite the many factors working against her, this really ended up being her lucky day. Ours is a busy Station and being out on a call isn't unusual. The unusual part is that on the call we were so close to the engine. It was good luck that I saw the call on the screen, that of all the rooms she could have been in we were able to find her quickly, that we had a thermal imager and that her room held the flames at bay long enough for us to find her. Yes indeed, It really was her lucky day.

I am very proud to say, that in my over 30 years of service, this was my first living life save at a fire. Our Department decorated the team and very proudly, we were awarded a Company Citation in the 2011 Firehouse Magazine Heroism Awards. I high point of my career.

HORSING AROUND
Captain Paul Youdelis - Station 12, C Platoon
Clark County Fire Department, Las Vegas, Nevada

When the winds pay Vegas a visit, the come in force and will rival the "Windy City" Chicago. When the winds do roll in, Firefighters across the Valley dread the notion of a fire.

This shift, the wind rolled in during the early evening and the usual hell broke loose. signal calls, wires down and such. Calls started to flow. We had been running pretty steadily, when we were dispatched out to a report of a fire in a corral.

We were a bit out, so other units were arriving ahead of us. As they began arriving they found more than just some fence burning. An entire barn type area, covered horse stalls hay and fencing were blazing away. In one central area, you could make out through the smoke and flames the bodies of deceased horses, but more disturbing was the image of the one horse still standing.

The poor creature was trapped by a fence on one side and a wall of flames on three other sides. You couldn't see it from where my company initially was positioned, but the frightened animal had been burned and was clearly in distress. Battalion Chief RB Taylor called my company up. We met briefly and he asked me to take my crew and to see if there was anything we could do to help the trapped horse.

I had my crew quickly pull an attack line and we began fighting our way through the fire while intermittently rain dropping water down onto the poor horse. Between the smoke, the fire, and the dirt whipping around in the 50 MPH wind gusts, the going was miserable. We blocked out the image of the burned, dead horses and stayed focused on the prize, the still living animal, hoping it wouldn't bolt and perish.

The horse remained pressed against the fence as we worked our way to it. Perhaps it knew we were trying to help, or maybe it was immobile from fear, either way, we were happy that the horse was helping us out by staying put. We circled around the animal and hoped that if it finally bolted, it would run back they way we had come.

I'm not a horse guy, but I was determined to help this magnificent animal. I took off my mask and helmet so it could recognize me as a human and approached slowly, talking soothingly to it. I'm not sure who was more frightened at this point. I was honestly terrified. Visions of a horse tap dancing on my skull were running through my brain.

The horse had some kind of horse hardware on him with some straps. I gently grabbed them and lead the horse along the safe path being cut by my crew. After finding an open, safe area, I quickly handed off the horse to a "Horse wise" bystander and was happy to do so. It was late and no vets were to be find, so we got the Metropolitan Police Department to send out their mounted units vet to help.

This was a different kind of life save, but one that continues to bring a smile to my face when I think back on it. It was one of my proudest moments.

PARAMEDIC PENIS

Captain Paul Youdelis - Station 12, C Platoon
Clark County Fire Department, Las Vegas, Nevada

The young man standing in his hotel room surrounded by Fire and Ambulance personnel seemed nonplussed to describe his medical problem. He had a sore spot on his penis like a a minor burn or a scrape. "I just need a Paramedic to take a look at it" he announced.

The four Firefighters and two Medics from the ambulance company started to look around at each other, with all eyes landing on the one Medic from the Ambulance - The one to have the misfortune to have the words "PARAMEDIC" emblazoned on the front of his shirt.

Some one blurted out, "Looks like you got this one".

KATRINA

Captain Paul Youdelis - Station 12, C Platoon
Clark County Fire Department, Las Vegas, Nevada

The Clark County Fire Department is one of the Countries chosen entities to host a FEMA Urban Search and Rescue Team. Many of the our department members, myself included signed up for this extra duty. Members of this elite team (NVTF-1) receive advanced training in various emergency disciplines and have an equipment cache designed to square off with any disaster.

NVTF-1 along with many other task forces were put on alert as Hurricane Katrina approached the Louisiana coast. Some teams began to move up in anticipation while others prepared to depart. Shortly after the true enormity of the disaster was realized, NVTF-1 was deployed and began the long, non-stop trek from Nevada to the coast. Arriving teams were given many different assignments. Some went to Mississippi while others went to Louisiana and specifically New Orleans. Our team was held back to relive the initial arriving units.

After staging just outside of the disaster area, we finally received orders to advance and relieve teams in the City of New Orleans. We moved up to the New Orleans Saints practice facilities where teams were maintaing their BOO. We rapidly set up our facilities and prepared for a mission the following day.

We were sent out the next day to conduct secondary searches of homes in the Eastern part of the city that bordered on Lake Pontchartrain. A painful lesson learned is that the Urban Search and Rescue Teams were woefully unprepared for water operations having no boats in the equipment cache. Boats were certainly going to be a problem for us... at first.

I had previously been deployed to the World Trade Center. I clearly remember thinking as I stood a Ground Zero, this was as bad as it gets.

I would never see anything worse in my life. I was wrong. Every inch of New Orleans and its surrounding communities was under five to fifteen feet of water. Everything! As far as the eye could see! Even from the lofty vantage point of a military Chinook helicopter. I learned from my past mistake and didn't say it cant get any worse, but this was seriously beyond human comprehension.

We got to our search area and were joined by two Coast Guard teams that had small boats. From the group, we made two small squads who made there way out, leaving the rest of the team to find ways to make themselves useful. Many of the fleeing residents did so in their own boats, which were left scattered on every visible spot of dry land. These craft were quickly made targets. Viable boats, batteries, and outboard motors were confiscated and turned into our own little armada.

With our makeshift fleet, we now had many squads conducting searches, and began to make quick work of our assigned area, saddened to only find corpses. As disheartening as the task seemed to be at the time, everyone pushed on Several days into our secondary searches, the sun finally shone on NVTF-1. A crew began a search of a house and amazingly found a survivor!

Searching these homes was precarious at best. The boat was moved up against the house and a ladder was raised from inside the boat, to a high point of the home that was above the water line. Like circus performers, rescuers would scramble up the unstable ladder and force entry into the building. In this case, crews had made their way onto the roof, noticing signs that someone may have been in there. The team cut their way into the attic.

Following emergency instructions that most residents of New Orleans knew, the Elderly couple who lived at the home made their way to the attic when the floods came. This would prove for many to be a fatal mistake.

Tragically, the pair found themselves hopelessly trapped in the attic. As time passed, the mans wife passed away. He remained by her side, clinging to life and hope all while mourning for his wife. The man was close to the grim reaper himself when NVTF-1 stepped foot onto his roof. Every member of the Task Force lamented the passing of his wife, but were heartened to find at least the man alive. To my knowledge, this was the last survivor pulled out of New Orleans. It made the entire, grueling trip worth it.

I TOLD YOU I'D DO IT!
Captain Paul Youdelis - Station 12, C Platoon
Clark County Fire Department, Las Vegas, Nevada

We were dispatched to the now non-existent, Frontier Hotel's parking lot to assist Metro with a suicidal man. We arrived and met with officers who told us there was a man locked inside his van, he had poured gasoline all over himself and was threatening the light himself on fire.

I discussed the situation with the officers and a plan was devised while my crew pulled a hose line in case he lit up. The plan was that the officers would distract the man from the front of the van while we positioned our selves on either side from the rear. One fire fighter would pop the passenger side window with a spring loaded center punch and the other firefighter would immediately hit him through the broken window with a full water barrage from our hose line. We positioned another firefighter on the drivers side with an axe to take that window out right after we doused the man so Metro could get to him.

We all moved into position and Metro began talking to the distraught man, positioning themselves so there was less of chance of him seeing us. The timing was perfect. The first firefighter clicked the spring loaded center punch on the window and his back up yanked back on the bale of the nozzle to hit the suicidal man full stream. The problem was, the window didn't break!

The center punch for some reason failed to break the glass on the first shot, and the water stream was just ricocheting off the window. Almost simultaneously there was a loud "Whooomp" sound. The man had flicked his Bic and all the fumes that had filled the van from his gasoline soaked clothes explosively flashed and the man began to burn. He was screaming and howling as if he were being incinerated. The firefighter on the other side took the drivers side window out with the axe and on the passenger side a second attempt from the center punch proved successful.

the water stream was now able to extinguish the burning man and officers reached in, unlocked the door, and snatched the man out of the now smoldering, smoking vehicle.

In the end, the man suffered very minor burns. It seemed that all of this happened faster then it felt like in real life, and only the gasoline on his body really burned. He was handcuffed and treated in preparation for a ride to the hospital, all the while he simply boasted, " told you I'd do it! I told you! See! I did it!"

World Trade Center

Captain Paul Youdelis - Station 12, C Platoon
Clark County Fire Department, Las Vegas, Nevada

As a member of FEMA's Urban Search And Rescue Team, NVTF-1 which is sponsored by the Clark County Fire Department, I had little doubt the Task Force would be deployed when cowards attacked America on September 11th, 2001.

I, like the rest of the Country woke to the horrific news. America was under attack. I watched the television along with the rest of the Country, horrified by the disasters in Pennsylvania, Washington DC, and New York. There was no doubt in my mind, that a lot of people had, and would die, and when the Towers fell, I knew in my soul that a lot of firefighters had fallen with them.

I felt sick. My heart was suffering, but my mind was in high gear. I knew every FEMA Team in the Country would be deployed over the next couple of weeks, and I had work to do.

I gathered all my mobility gear and began to double check it. I wanted to be sure to have everything right. Anger was pushing out sorrow and I wanted to get in the game. Word came down that we would be held in reserve should something else happen and then deployed later in the week as a relief team. It was going to be a long week.

We tried to make the most of the week, reviewing our cache of equipment, and ensuring all team members were ready to go so that when the word came down we could jet. That word finally came, and we were on our way, ready to do our part.

We arrived in New York and were shuttled to the Javitts Center where all the teams were bivouacked. We worked efficiently, setting up our BOO, and prepared for our first shift out at the site.

Morning came, and many of us were up early with duties that needed to be accomplished before the team headed to ground zero. Time passed, and soon the team was on the bus looking out the windows to see a New York covered in thick dust and streets clogged with debris and litter. All of the foreshadowing of what we would soon see.

The bus had to drop our team short of the site because of all the recovery and rescue vehicles, not to mention the increasing amounts of debris. We got off the bus and hiked in to the site. My immediate impression was one of utter disbelief. In the heart of one of the greatest cities in the world was a place where proud skyscrapers had once been, replaced by a fuming pile of rubble and death. Our hearts sank again as if the attacks had just happened. How could mankind do this to one another?

Over a week had passed since the attack, and yet the place look to us as if it had happened just hours ago. Someone had mentioned to us that everything was so much better. The very area where we were standing had just a few short days prior been under almost 15 feet of debris.

It took a while for us to get an assignment. Stress levels were high for the New Yorkers and members of the FDNY. In their zeal to help, many individuals and groups flocked to the site and just made their way out to the rubble pile with out permission, so all new comers were looked on with a wary eye. Our K-9 teams were put to use fairly quickly and did such a great job, that our team earned a place in the mission and soon tasks began to flow.

We had been given an assignment to complete a secondary search of an imposing high rise with a huge, knife like gash slashed into its side. We gathered our belongings and were preparing to move out when I noticed the strange pile of shredded ring type objects. As we marched passed, It dawned on me that this was a massive pile of shattered fiberglass air bottles from firefighters SCBA, that was being recovered from the pile. That pile of fiberglass represented firefighters who had been trapped in the collapsing buildings. That pile represented heroism.

Despite our best efforts and deepest hopes, There was no one left alive to rescue. Our team ended up providing logistical support, Equipment, technical advice and most importantly K-9 services. The most viivd memory I'll have of our efforts at ground zero came when our K-9's and search teams found the remains of a New York City Firefighter.

The dogs alerted and the search team moved in. The team made notifications that they had found a fallen hero. All work on the pile stopped and the site became oddly, comparatively silent. A team of of FDNY Firefighters moved in to collect their fallen brother. They had solemn, tired faces. The strain of the past days had clearly taken their toll, yet it was clear from the look in there determined eyes, that they, and no one else would tend to their fallen brother. As I write this and remember my eyes are filling with tears.

The team plodded over the pile to their brother and with absolute respect moved the hero to a stokes basket. One firefighter produced a flag that they had taken out to their brother and respectfully covered him. As they escorted him off the pile, heads bowed and salutes were given to honor one of New York's bravest. It is sad to say, that this operation was repeated far to many times in the days following the attacks.

I realized that I would never forget my time at ground zero, and also thought, that that would be a good thing. I shouldn't forget. We shouldn't forget.

MOUSE
Captain Paul Youdelis - Station 12, C Platoon
Clark County Fire Department, Las Vegas, Nevada

Mouse. A true thorn in our side. If there was ever a customer who tested our professionalism it would have to have been Mouse.

Mouse was a vagrant who chose to center his world in the middle of our part of the Las Vegas Strip. This was a bad thing. A very bad thing. You could count on seeing Mouse at least once during almost every shift. There were times where Mouse would call 911 several times during the day.

Mouse's favorite game was to call 911 reporting he had been hit by a car. This advance level call automatically dispatched not just one unit, but a fire engine, a rescue unit, an ambulance, and several police units. On arrival, the story would be that this had happened some time ago and that he was now in pain. Mouse may not have known much, but he did know that the hospital had a bed he could sleep in and free food. Mouse was very good at playing his game.

Indeed, Mouse was very good at playing his game, but to us it wasn't a game. While units were tied up with Mouse, calls for people in real need were missed and sorely needed hospital beds were tied up.

On this particular shift, we were seeing Mouse for the third time and we hadn't even been on duty for 12 hours yet. In fact, Mouse still had hospital bracelets on his wrists from earlier in the day. I had lost my patience with him, so I requested Metro PD to continue in and my crew to evaluate him. He was of course apparently fine.

The officer arrived and started to deal with Mouse telling him that this abuse needed to stop. We all realized that this was probably pointless. As the Officer continued to talk to Mouse one of my Crew members leaned over to me and whispered, "Mouse better hope there's no such thing as Karma. If there is, one day he's gonna get hit by a car for real!"

The Cop finished with Mouse and we transported him again to the hospital, hoping this would be the last time we would see him this shift.

Later that shift, we had just finished dinner when we were toned out for an Auto/Ped off the Strip. We ran hot to the call and as we approached we could see a body wadded up in the middle of the busy commercial street. When we got close enough, one of my firefighters exclaimed, "Cap! That's Mouse!" Sure enough, next to the critically injured man was the easily recognizable, dirty orange hat - A trademark of Mouse's

It would seem that, Karma did indeed get Mouse. He had just been again released from the hospital from that last call, immediately started drinking, and stumbled out into to busy thoroughfare and was blasted by a fast moving car. Needless to say, we went about our business trying to save Mouse's life to the very best of our abilities, as if he were anyone else, all with a shocked, creeped out look on our faces!

ASSORTED RUN NOTES...

Captain Paul Youdelis - Station 12, C Platoon
   Clark County Fire Department, Las Vegas, Nevada
   These simple short notes are just a sampling if the classic notes we
can find on the initial dispatch.

Notes:
   45 YOF CB... BLOOD CLOTS FROM RECTUM BLEEDING
THROUGH CLOTHES
   Notes:
   55 YOM LIGHTING A CIGARETTE IN THE WIND LIT
HIS HAIR, EAR, & EYE ON FIRE
   PAT IS C/B
   FIRE IS OUT NOW BUT PAT HAS BURNS TO HEAD AND
FACE
   Notes:
   TOW TRUCK W/ NAKED WMA... PENIS WRAPPED IN
PLASTIC... IN PAIN...
   PT STATES SOMEONE CUT HIS CLOTHES OFF AND
TIED SOMETHING AROUND HIS PENIS
   Notes:
   32 YOM C/B BELIEVES WIFE POURED CHEMICALS
AND BLACK DUST ALL OVER COUNTERS IN KITCHEN
AND INSIDE HOME
   PR STATES GIRLFRIEND PUT A CHEMICAL INSIDE
VAGINA AND MADE LOVE TO BOYFRIEND, SMELLS LIKE
GASOLINE
   Notes:

40 YOM 408... CRAWLING WITH A BEER... SAYS HE IS TRYING TO GET HOME... BUT THINKS HE BROKE HIS LEG UNKNOWN WHAT HAPPENED

Notes:

SOMEONE CHOKING AT JOE'S CRAB SHACK

PER MANAGER PT WAS NOT CHOKING, HE WAS OVERWHELMED WITH THE CONVERSATION AT THE TABLE, STARTED TO P/O, WANTS TO BE CHECKED

Notes:

63 YOM C/B WAS HAVING RELATIONS WITH WIFE NOW HAVING PENIS PAIN

Notes:

33 YOF CON/B CRYING FOR 3 DAYS

Notes:

17 YOF C/B, PUT... TAMPAX IN AND LOST IT NEEDS HELP GETTING IT OUT

Notes:

MASSAGE PARLOR, PR WALKED BY, HEARING SCREAMING / THUMPS

Notes:

22 YOM... CAB... PENIS PROBLEMS

Notes:

31 YOM C/B CUT RECTAL AREA ATTEMPTING TO SHAVE HIMSELF

Notes:

25 YOM C/B INJ TO EYE FROM ROULETTE BALL

Notes:

NON VIOLENT NO WEPONS HOTEL MANAGER IS 97

SAYS SHE IS SARA CONNER FROM THE TERMINATOR

FEMALE IN THE LOBBY 30ISH YOF C/B PT THINKS SHE IS FROM THE MOVIE TERMINATOR SPEAKING IN UNKOWN LANGUAGE

GLOSSARY

14 GAUGE NEEDLE: A larger bore, needle used in giving IV Therapy.

1 3/4" LINE: The most commonly used fire attack line.

2 1/2" LINE: Fire hose most often used on larger fires.

AFFF: Aqueous Film Forming Foam: Foam used to extinguish fuel fires.

ALARMS: Most often called First, Second, Third, Fourth, and Fifth Alarms. While this can vary from department to department, each alarm doubles the number of units that respond to a scene. A Second Alarm would have twice as many units as a single alarm.

ALS UNIT: Advanced life support Unit. Rescue company which is manned with a Paramedic.

AMONIUM PERCHLORATE: A product used in the manufacture of rocket fuel. An oxidizer.

AORTA: A major artery that comes off of the heart.

APNIC: Not breathing

ASSESSMENT: Primary/Secondary. To determine the extent of a patients injury.

BAGGING: Ventilating a patient with a bag valve mask

BAG VALVE MASK: Resuscitation device, used to ventilate patients.

BATTALION CHIEF: Line officer usually in command of several stations and Captains. Most often commands at fire scenes. A promoted position.

BLEVE: Acronym for Boiling Liquid Expanding Vapor Explosion. Violent, devastating explosion brought on by the sudden rupture of a liquefied gas container.

BLS UNIT: Basic Life Support Unit. Emergency vehicle manned by EMT's. A step below an ALS Unit.

BOOSTER LINE: Small line used for nuisance fires.

CANNULA: Small tube used to administer oxygen through the nose.

CAPTAIN: In charge of an individual Fire Company. A promoted position. Most often will have an Engineer and two Fire Fighters under his command. Will at times take command of a fire, or make initial attack with his crew.

CLACKER: A wooden noise maker used by fire watches to wake the town when they discovered a blaze.

CODE: Victim with no pulse, respirations, or blood pressure.

CPR: Cardio Pulmonary Resuscitation. A life saving technique everyone should know to keep blood from pumping in the body and oxygenating the brain.

CRITICAL STRESS: Condition that can often effect Emergency Workers who are trying to deal with extreme situations.

DEFIBRILLATOR: Device used to shock the heart into viable rhythm.

EMERGENCY COMMUNICATIONS CENTER: Dispatchers, who answer 911 calls, assign units, and handle radio traffic.

EMS/EMERGENCY MEDICAL SERVICES: Field Medics such as Paramedics and Emergency Medical Technicians

EMT: Emergency Medical Technician. An EMS provider at a lower skill level than a paramedic.

ENGINE/ENGINE COMPANY: A fire vehicle with the primary function of supplying hose and water to extinguish the fire. Usually manned by a Captain, Engineer, and Two Fire Fighters.

ENGINEER: The fire fighter who drives the Engine or Truck. Most often a promoted position. Also called a Chauffeur.

EXPLORER: An advanced form of scouting which focuses on careers.

FIRE FIGHTER: A line member of a fire department, also a position/rank. After Rookie, you become a fire fighter. Fire fighters pull the hose lines, place ladders, etc.

FIRST DEGREE BURN: A burn equal to a sunburn. Not considered very serious.

FRENCH TICKLER: Well, I guess I don't need to clarify that.

FULL ARREST: A code. No pulse, respirations, or blood pressure.

FUSIBLE LINK: Small metal device that keeps sprinkler heads closed. Heat from fire triggers them allowing the sprinkler head to open.

HOLDING C SPINE: To maintain the anatomical position of the head and neck in cases of suspected cervical injury.

HOUSELINES: Fire hose kept in a cabinet of building for fire department use.

HYPOTHERMIA: medical situation where the victims body temperature is to low.

IV: A set up to deliver fluids Intravenously

JAWS: The Hurst tool or "Jaws of Life"

JUMPER: A suicide attempt made by a person trying to jump from an elevated position (Most often the roof/ledge of a building)

KLING: A type of gauze that adheres to itself.

LADDER TRUCK: Vehicle with primary function of ladder work. Carries large truck mounted ladder, and full compliment of ground ladders.

LIFEPAK: Heart monitor and defibrillator.

LITTLE GIANT LADDER: Multi function ladder that can be formed into various shapes.

MASKED UP: To put on (Start using) Self Contained Breathing Apparatus.

MED BAGS: Medical Bags. The usual compliment includes an airway bag, drug bag, and defibrillator.

OVERHAUL: After the fire is out, fire fighters overhaul, looking for small hidden fires, smoldering embers, and insuring that the fire is completely out. A fire that rekindles is an embarrassment to fire crews.

PARAMEDIC: EMS worker trained in advanced Life support. Many fire fighters are paramedics. They may administer certain types of drugs and have other advance life saving skills.

PERSONAL FLOTATION DEVICE: Life jacket

PIKE POLE: Long pole with a point and hook on the end. Used for removing windows and pulling ceilings.

PRECONNECT: A line attached to a discharge of the engine ready for immediate use.

PRIMARY LIFE SEARCH: A rapid search of a fire building for victims.

PROBIE: Probationary fire fighter, or rookie

PRONOUNCED: To be pronounced dead.

PUMPER: A fire engine.

RADIAL PULSE: Pulse found at the wrist.

RAPPELLING: Working down sheer cliffs/building faces on ropes.

REGULATOR: Device used to control air flow on the SCBA

REHAB: To cool down/take a break.

RHYTHM: Heart rhythm as shown on a monitor.

RIG: A piece of fire apparatus.

SCBA/SELF CONTAINED BREATHING APPARATUS: The airpack and mask fire fighters wear to provide breathable air.

SECONDARY LIFE SEARCH: A second, slower, more thorough search of a fire building for victims.

SECOND DEGREE BURN: A burn more sever than first, which includes blistering and peeling of the skin.

SOB: Short of Breath

SPRINKLER HEAD: End of sprinkler system designed to distribute water in an effective fire fighting pattern.

STETHOSCOPE: Device used in the to amplify sound, used for taking blood pressure, listening to lung sounds, and the heart.

STICK: A Ladder on a ladder truck.

SUPPLY LINE: Hose laid from the fire hydrant to the fire engine.

TAPPED OUT: Fire fighter used to be dispatched through a series of bell rings sent to them over a telegraph. The bell would "Tap Out" a number of rings, indicating where the call was. The term is sometimes used to refer to being dispatched today.

THE FLOOR: Slang meaning active duty on a fire department (Suppression)

THIRD DEGREE BURN: The most sever types of burns. Skin is charred. These burns can prove to be fatal.

TRAUMA: Injury sustained through force.

TRIPOD POSITION: On hands and knees, sitting on the heels of the feet.

TURNOUTS: The protective suit fire fighters wear, also called Bunker Gear.

VENTILATE: The act of removing products of combustion from a fire building.

WASHDOWN: To use the on board water to wash down gas, oil, blood, etc.

WYE: An appliance used to split one hose line into two.

The stories depicted here are the sole memory of the the submitters and are not official tales of any responses. The stories are not about an specific person or persons. Any likeness to an individual or their situation is strictly coincidental.

About the Author

Paul Youdelis is currently in the employ of the Clark County Fire Department as a Company Officer with over 17 years experiencein his current position, 25 years with Clark County and in excess of 30 years cumulative experience in thefire service.For the last 16 years, he has been the Company Officer at Fire Station 12 - C Platoon, and has the longest running tenure on the Las Vegas Strip of any department member currently servicing that area.In his time at Station 12, he has had the opportunity to function in many command roles from a Company level to IncidentCommander at emergency calls big and small. He has accumulated real life experience an almost all aspects of the fire service such as Structural Fire Operations, CFR (Crash-Fire-Rescue), Emergency Medicine, Dispatching, Training, and Fire Prevention.The fire service is his love, but his family is his life. Away from the Clark County Fire Department his world revolves around his wonderful wife and four fantastic kids. He has been married to his love, Reggi for 24 yearsand has two sons and two daughters. His boys are both enrolled at UNLV and work with the Rebel FootballTeam. His two daughters have branched out on their own and have jobs in Colorado Springs, Colorado.He also enjoys Photography, writing, computers and woodworking